Character

MAKE-UP

by Paul Thompson and Gil Romero

First Printing 2008

ISBN13: 978-0-9802318-5-4

Library of Congress Control Number: 2008930020

For information, please contact:
Make-up Designory®
129 S. San Fernando Boulevard
Burbank, CA 91502
818-729-9420

Acknowledgments

First and foremost, we wish to thank the students, whose thirst for knowledge
has led us to develop and create the curriculum and techniques
that are designed to reach the artist in all of them.
Without them, we would not have had the
dedication to complete this book.

In addition, we would like to thank everyone who
has contributed or helped make this book a reality.
A heartfelt thank you goes to Tate Holland, John Bailey,
Karl Zundel, Peter Lambertz, Monique Barrett, Kumara Luly,
Francine Reich, Michele Mulkey, Myles O'Reilly, Derek Althen,
Tara Holland, Stephanie Caillabet, Juliet Loveland and Aniko Hill.

We dedicate this book to our children Samantha, Emma and Valan.

TABLE OF CONTENTS

TABLE OF CONTENTS

PREFACE

Introduction to Character Make-up

Make-up artistry is the art of changing or beautifying the face. A make-up artist is a person that creates or changes the look of an actor, model or individual. They typically work in the theater, film, television, and fashion industries; however there are an increasing number of opportunities available. Make-up application has been around for thousands of years; people all over the world have used some type of make-up to alter their personal appearance. In addition, make-up has been used in theater for hundreds of years to create a variety of characters that was primarily applied by the performers.

The process of showing a recorded image was developed in the 1860's. In 1893 at the Chicago World Fair, Thomas Edison introduced to the public two pioneering inventions: the Kinetograph, the first practical moving picture camera, and the Kinetoscope, a cabinet with a continuous loop of Dickson's celluloid film. Dickson supplied Kinetoscope parlors with fifty-foot film snippets, photographed in Edison's "Black Maria" studio. These sequences recorded entertainment acts like acrobats, music hall performers, and boxing demonstrations. The movies of the time were seen mostly in temporary storefront spaces and traveling exhibitions. A film could be under a minute long and would usually present a single scene, authentic or staged, of everyday life: a public event, a sporting event, or slapstick. There were little or no cinematic

techniques employed. There was no editing and usually no camera movement, but the novelty of realistically-moving photographs was enough for a motion picture industry to mushroom before the end of the century. Paris stage magician Georges Melies began shooting and exhibiting films in 1896. His films mainly involved fantasy and the bizarre, including *A Trip to the Moon* in 1902. He pioneered many of the fundamental special effects techniques used in movies for most of the twentieth century, demonstrating that film had the power to distort visual reality rather than just faithfully recording it. He also led the way in making multi-scene narratives as long as fifteen minutes.

During the early years of film actors did their own make-up as they had done for theater. The first pioneer in make-up was an actor named Lon Chaney, who was dubbed, "the man of a thousand faces," because of his ability to transform himself using self-invented make-up techniques for almost every one of his characters. He entered a stage career in 1902, and began travelling with popular Vaudeville and theater acts. Chaney is chiefly remembered as a pioneer in such silent horror films as *The Hunchback of Notre Dame* and most notably *The Phantom of the Opera*. In an autobiographical 1925 article published in *Movie* magazine, Chaney referred to his specialty as "extreme characterization". Every make-up created can be considered a character make-up, whether it is a strange alien creation or a model selling the latest apparel in a fashion magazine.

In the 1920's, George Westmore, a hairdresser who emigrated to the United States with his family, was known for establishing the first movie make-up department. Would-be make-up artists during this time would apprentice with veteran artists to learn the trade. The apprenticeship program was used by the studios to train newcomers in all technical trades including make-up. The studio system was a means of film production and distribution dominant in Hollywood from the early 1920's through the early 1950's. The term "studio system" refers to the practice of large motion picture studios producing movies primarily on their own filmmaking lots with creative personnel under long-term contract and having ownership or effective control of distributors and movie theaters. A 1948 Supreme Court ruling against those distribution and exhibition practices brought an end to the studio system. In 1954, the last of the operational links between a major production studio and theater chain was broken and the era of the studio system was officially dead. As a result, the studio departments started to disappear. Performers and creative personnel were contracted for the length of a particular film. By the mid 1960s, the apprenticeship program for make-up artists was almost non-existent. Vocational make-up schools eventually picked up where the apprenticeship program left off and taught out-of-the-kit techniques employed by make-up artists to all that wanted to learn. Make-up techniques largely remained the same for most of the twentieth century. In the last twenty years there has been a surge of new advances in materials and techniques, mainly because the audience and broadcast systems have become more sophisticated.

The make-up profession offers an artist many options from working in the fashion industry doing make-up on beautiful models to creating yet-to-be imagined characters for the film screen. Giving an artist the rare opportunity to work in a collaborative environment creating characters that have the potential to become part of popular culture. This book is a step-by-step guide to different types of character make-ups, with the emphasis on what we would call special make-up effects rather than on beauty techniques. We are not only teaching how to be a make-up artist, but also how to think like one. Realize it would be impossible for us to include in this book the infinite possibilities faced by make-up artists. Instead, an artist will be able to build upon and grow from the included techniques. This book is written on the principle that each chapter builds on the previous chapter. We start with the basics of being an artist and how to think properly and finish with the focus on the application of make-up to an actor. Make-up artistry is a very demanding subject, and requires total dedication to both practicing the techniques and the quest for more knowledge. We suggest practicing each technique immediately following the chapter to gain a better understanding of the material. The book uses photographs to highlight each process, which makes it very easy to follow and allows the book to be used as a reference when attempting each technique. We also touch on how prosthetics are made and formulated, but only as an overview rather than as a how-to. The industry is ever changing and a good artist must stay informed and accept the changes that inevitably will happen.

CHAPTER 1

Make-up Principles

The Artist

Art is a very diverse subject that encompasses numerous preconceived notions of what an artist is. Many people feel that art is an inherent talent, and artists are born with some magical gift that allows them to do what they do, when in reality art is a learned skill that is developed into well-executed skills. Although some geniuses do exist, such as Leonardo da Vinci and Michelangelo, most artists are very well practiced normal people. We all start out in life seeing and working as artists, but somewhere in adolescence we stop drawing or painting and start believing that we are not artistic. The people that continue to work through their childhood are the artists most people feel have that magical talent. These skills can be learned at any point in life, regardless of age. With enough perseverance and lots of practice you can achieve your goals, whether they are to be an artist or a make-up artist.

Highlight and Shadow

Highlight and shadow, otherwise known as shading, is everything to an artist. In order to understand this concept we must begin to think and see as an artist. A great book about this subject is "Drawing on the Right Side of the Brain" by Betty Edwards. She does not mean drawing on the correct side of the brain, but rather she has identified a region of the brain that controls creativity and artistic abilities. The left side of the brain controls communication, mathematics, and anything analytical, while the right side of the brain controls creativity. The basic concept of the book is not how to draw but how to see. Most people do not draw what they see; they usually draw what they think they can draw. The book helps to break these bad habits and shows the reader how to really look at an object and draw what is being viewed. It also trains the brain to slip into the creative mode, allowing the artist to think artistically. Art is a learned skill that can be successfully executed by just about anyone. Look at a photograph of a face and focus on the nose, carefully look at the nose and visualize the shapes that make it up. Throw out those useless terms that are used to communicate and replace them with just what is seen. Understand that the object formerly known as the nose is curved here and straight there, it has roundness and looks a bit cylindrical.

Classically speaking, the only way to achieve a three-dimensional appearance is with shading. In fact, every make-up done, even beauty make-up, is nothing more than a brilliant execution of highlight and shadow. While drawing, an artist uses shading to create the illusion of depth. This is done by applying media more densely or using a darker media for darker areas and applying media lightly or using a lighter media for lighter areas. The same applies for make-up; well-placed shadows can depress an area of the face and conversely, a well-placed highlight can pull an area of the face forward. The shadow and the highlight should be layered to create the illusion of depth. Understanding these basic principles of shading and how they affect different objects and surfaces is the key to a successful drawing or make-up application.

Sculptural Light

An artist that paints portraits selects the light source for the painting and positions it anywhere desired. This doesn't mean there is a lamp painted in the picture; it means the face is shaded according to the position of the light. If the light source is not followed then the painting will not look very real. Make-up artists are faced with a similar situation; however the light source cannot be arbitrarily placed. Since the performer is moving around in a three-dimensional world the shading needs to be done a very specific way. The highlights and shadows must be painted on the performer as if the light is above and in front of the performer. This will allow the shading to work no matter which angle it was viewed from and without having to worry about where the actual lights on set are placed. So when asked where to place a highlight or a shadow, the answer lies within another question: where is the light? Once the light source is identified (always above and in front of the actor) it is easy to decide where to paint the highlight and shadows. This concept is probably the most understated concept in make-up, yet it is absolutely essential to proper placement of highlights and shadows. It is the difference between an okay make-up and a great make-up.

The Two-Dimensional World

There is a difference between the three-dimensional world and the two-dimensional world of film and television. Look into a mirror and notice that your image is really flat and shapeless. You are seeing yourself two-dimensionally. Next, hold a finger in front of your face and close one eye, then open that eye and close the other. Your finger will move from side to side as you switch eyes. This happens because we have two eyes enabling us to see the same object from two different perspectives. This is why humans can tell depth and see how far away an object is from the viewer. Height, width and depth are the three-dimensions. With this knowledge we are able to make three-dimensional movies. This technique usually involves filming a single object with two cameras. When viewed, usually wearing the funny glasses, each eye sees its photographed counterpart. The visual cortex interprets the pair of images as a single three-dimensional image. A regular camera records everything through one lens and is projected onto a flat wall or shown on a flat screen and is why film and television are two-dimensional. We do not have the ability to tell depth. What this means for a make-up artist is that we can fool the audience into believing they are seeing something that may only be painted on the face as opposed to really being there. They do not have the ability to really see the depth but rather the illusion of depth created by us.

Color

As artists we must have a firm understanding of color, sometimes viewed as a magical element that only gifted artists are able to grasp. There are three basic aspects of color: hue, value (lightness), and chroma (color purity or colorfulness). Professor Albert H. Munsell created this system. The system consists of three independent dimensions, which can be represented cylindrically as an irregular color solid. Hue is the name of the color and is measured by degrees around a horizontal circle. Value pertains to how light or dark a color looks or the amount of white or black is added to a color. Thus value is the amount of gray a color has in it. Chroma is measured outward from the neutral gray and refers to the purity of the color.

There are three primary colors: red, blue, and yellow. There are three secondary colors: red mixed with blue equals purple, blue mixed with yellow equals green, and yellow mixed with red equals orange. The color wheel is these colors arranged in a circle with the respective primaries between the proper secondary colors. Further, mix the secondary colors with the primaries to get another color between each secondary and primary. On the color wheel, the two colors directly across from each other are complimentary colors. White and black can now be added to every color to change the value of that color. White will make the original color lighter and less vibrant. Black does the opposite of white, making the color darker and less vibrant. In cosmetics we can apply these same rules to color. However, when mixing cosmetics there is less of a chance true primary or secondary colors are used. Normally, some form of primary colors is used so this color theory should be kept in mind when combining color for make-ups. Note that black is usually a really dark blue or green, when referring to cosmetics.

Sanitation

As a make-up artist, sanitation is a very important part of maintaining a clean and professional environment. The cleanliness of the artist and the station is the first step in conveying competence to an actor.

Always maintain a clean and neat appearance. Hand sanitizer should be at the station at all times and should be utilized between each actor. After eating or smoking, wash hands with soap and water and consider brushing teeth. All brushes should be cleaned with brush cleaner immediately after each use. Do not wait to clean the brushes until another actor is in the chair. Sponges and powder puffs should only be used on one performer and thrown away after each use. Some artists choose to maintain a sponge or a puff inside a Zip-lock bag for a single performer. This is acceptable as long as they are thrown away at the end of the day. Disposable mascara wands are just that, disposable, and should never be returned to a mascara container after touching any part of the face.

Combs and hairbrushes need to be chemically sanitized with Barbicide or bleach solution after each use. They are never to be used on more than one person without being sanitized. Remove hair from the comb or brush, rinse with water, and drop into either of the solutions. Barbicide comes in a concentrate and is diluted with water. The temperature of the water is not a factor. Follow the manufacturer's directions when mixing Barbicide with water. For the bleach solution, mix a quarter cup of bleach with one gallon of water. Again, the temperature of the water is not a factor. Both solutions are good for a twenty-four hour period and must be thrown out after that time. Leave combs and hairbrushes immersed for no less than ten minutes, then remove and rinse with clean water.

Make-up should be scooped from its container with a palette knife and placed onto a palette. Work from the palette, not from the container. The palette can be cleaned with 99% alcohol before working on the next performer. For pressed powders, where it is impossible to scoop out product, spritz the make-up with 99% alcohol to sanitize it. The nice thing about powder products is the low chance of bacteria growing in the container. A good rule of thumb is to remove the product from the container before applying it.

Pencils are sharpened to clean and then the sharpener can be cleaned with 99% alcohol. If anything falls onto the floor it is no longer sanitized and needs to be cleaned. This also goes for sneezing or coughing on an item.

Morgues

A morgue, for the make-up artist, is a vast reference book of pictures and photographs. It cannot be purchased it has to be built. Regardless of what area of make-up you are learning or interested in, the idea is to create a book of reference. It is a tool used when meeting to discuss concepts and designs with photographers, art directors, and/or directors. This morgue should be a book that is separate from any notes. Creating sections by using dividers in the book will help to organize the pictures into easy-to-find sections, however do this to your own liking. Categories could include, but are not limited to, men, women, children, elderly people, bald people, facial hair, hairstyles, monsters, animals, mythical characters, prosthetics, historical characters, wardrobe, critters, creatures, sculptures, statues, and injuries. Finding the pictures needed for a morgue is somewhat difficult. It will become an ongoing process where you will eventually fill a bookshelf as opposed to just one binder. Magazines and the Internet are great sources of pictures as well as newspapers. You may need to purchase specialty magazines to find specific photos, or you can go through your own magazines and pull the photos you need for specific sections.

Tools of the Trade

The following is the essential list of tools with a description of what each tool is required for and how it is used. These items are the tools you will be using to create just about every type of character make-up.

Brush Roll—Fabric brush holder that holds several brushes. It has a soft cover to help protect the bristle ends of the brushes and rolls into a tight roll for easy storage.

Brushes—A tool with hair or fibers imbedded into it, utilized for make-up application.

White Sponge—A soft foam latex sponge used to apply cream make-up.

Orange Sponge—A porous sponge used to apply cream make-up in a textured fashion.

Black Sponge—A heavily porous sponge used to apply cream make-up in a textured fashion. This sponge comes in three styles: fine, medium and coarse.

Palette Knife—A metal artist spatula used to scoop make-up out of a make-up container and to sculpt wax or blend an edge.

Tissue—A disposable piece of thin, soft, and absorbent paper.

Powder Puffs— A velour puff used to powder make-up. It helps absorb oils and create a shine-free finish.

Tweezers— Tools used for picking up small objects that are not easily handled with the hand. They can be used to remove hair or hold edges in place.

Mirror—A hand held mirror should be made available for the actors so they may see what you are doing throughout the process of making them up, especially if there is no large mirror at your disposal.

Scissors—You will need two pairs of scissors. A large, sharp pair of used for everything from cutting sponges to cutting into a bottle. These scissors should be very strong and durable. A second pair of small or more precise type of scissors is used for cutting hair or a bald cap. These should not be used as a general cutting tool and should not be used on sponges. Sponges dull scissors faster than anything else that a make-up artist may be cutting.

Comb—A standard barber comb can be used for a wide variety of situations from prepping hair for a bald cap to combing a fake beard. You may choose to purchase a set of combs to allow yourself a little variety and versatility.

Hair Brush—Mainly used on people with lots of hair. You may choose to purchase a set of brushes to allow yourself a little variety and versatility.

Cotton Swab—A stick with a small cotton ball on the end. Any type or style will do, however, we recommend the six-inch wooden handle swab. We find it more versatile than the average small swab.

Cotton Ball—Perfect for removing make-up or adhesive, it is one of the softest products you can use on a performer's face.

Make-up Pad—This is cotton pad used to remove make-up, and is used in a similar way to a cotton ball, with the exception it is a little more durable.

Make-up Box—A make-up kit. Can be made of wood, plastic, or aluminum. Each one has different features and it is completely a matter of personal choice and preference as to which one is best.

Set Bag—A medium sized bag usually having many side compartments for bottles and tools. It can also be a small individual bag used for the tools and touch up materials needed for only one performer.

Bald Cap Form—A life size plastic head used to create a bald cap. May be smooth or textured.

Container for Brush Cleaner—A small bottle with a lid used to clean brushes. This bottle is designed to be at the station with the contents being discarded at the end of each day.

Brush Holder—A plastic, metal, or glass cup to hold brushes upright.

Cotton Swab Holder—Same as a brush holder.

Hackle—A square piece of wood with metal spikes sticking out of it. It is used to detangle loose hair.

Utility Tweezers—A less expensive pair of tweezers used to tear latex on a burn.

Mints—Everyone needs fresh breath. Gum may irritate some performers.

Hand Sanitizer—Any professional sanitizer to clean hands.

Placemat—A disposable mat used to ensure a sanitary workspace.

Cover Cloth—A clean cloth that is used to protect the actor's wardrobe from accidental spills.

Make-up Pencil Sharpener—A metal sharpener, used to sharpen and sanitize your pencils.

Spray Bottle—Mainly for water, but can be used for just about any liquid. Use it to wet hair or make an actor look sweaty.

Hair Clip—Metal clip used to hold hair back and out of the way.

Hair Band—Coated rubber band to tie back hair.

Airbrush—A tool used to spray make-up onto a performer.

Compressor—A mechanical device used to supply air to the airbrush. A small silent type is best.

Pipe Cleaner—Used to clean small openings and parts on the airbrush.

Tooth Brush—Used to scrub paint off the airbrush, and can be used to flick texture onto a make-up.

Thinning Shears—Special scissors used to thin hair.

Curling Irons—Hot irons used to style hair. A variety of sizes are needed depending on the type of beard you are laying.

Metal Comb—Same as a standard barber comb except that it is made of metal and will not melt if touched by the curling iron.

Disposable Mascara Wand—A sanitary wand for applying mascara, it should be discarded after use.

Eyebrow Brush—A small brush to style the eyebrow and to clean make-up out of it.

1 oz. Plastic Cup—A thick plastic cup used for liquids. This cup enables small amount of liquid to be used at a time, allowing for double dipping.

Wide-Mouth Plastic Cup—Larger cup than the one ounce cup, allowing for larger objects (like a sponge) to be dipped into it.

Fingernail Clipper—For cutting nails. Nice to have for a performer if they need it.

10 cc. Syringe—A syringe without a needle used to dispense fake blood accurately.

Orange Wood Stick—A wooden stick that is beveled at both ends to form a wedge. It is normally used on cuticles, but can be adapted to just about any use.

Styptic Pencil—A small pencil looking object that will help stop the bleeding of small razor cuts.

Razor—An electric or disposable razor for those performers who need to shave. If you use the disposable type you will also need shaving cream; it is usually best to have both types.

Contact Lens Kit—A compact set that a performer can use to clean their contact lenses. Eye drops should be apart of this kit and can be used for dry eyes and irritation.

Student
Year

Kristy Tseng
2008

Student
Year

Joe Young Shim
2005

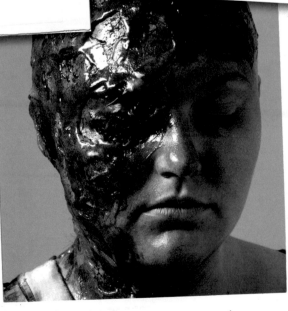

Student
Year

Cynthia Bergiadis
2006

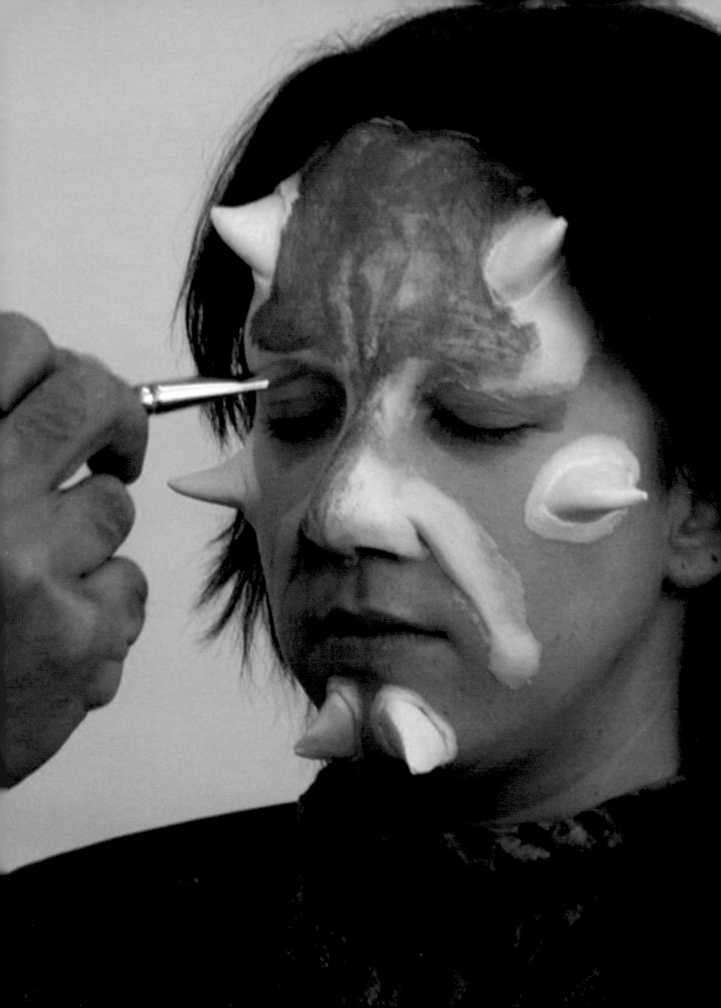

CHAPTER 2

Anatomy

Basic Structures of the Human Skull

A basic understanding of the skeletal features of the face is an important aspect of being a make-up artist. It is not important to commit all of this information to memory, but rather look at this as an overview that can be referenced whenever necessary. Only a few bone structures are important to recognize and identify as artists. These bone structures are often accentuated or softened, as artists try to define or reshape the human face. The human skull is comprised of 14 facial bones, 8 cranial bones, and 6 ear bones.

The facial bones support and shape the face, and provide the framework for the features of the face. Several of these bones form the smaller cavities within the skull, and are necessary to support the functions of the eyes, nose, inner ear and mouth. Facial bones are also key factors to the unique size and shape of each individual face. For all practical purposes, understanding the placement and function of these facial bones, which include the mandible, maxillae, zygomatic, and nasal bone, is fundamentally important.

The mandible, or mandibula in most other invertebrates, is commonly referred to as the jawbone. It is the only articulated bone in the adult human skull and is the largest and strongest facial bone. The maxillae are actually an ossified formation of several small facial bones. They form the second largest bone of the face and the upper jaw in its entirety. The maxillae extend to each zygomatic bone and rise to form a small lower part of the eye cavity, then continues further upward to the highest part of the nose. The zygomatic or malar bone forms the bony protrusion of the cheek. The zygomatic arch or process extends toward the grouping of the temporal fossa above the external acoustic meatus or external ear cavity. The nasal bone is actually comprised of two smaller, oblong bones, which form the rectangular plane of the nose bridge. The cranial bones form the calvarium. It is the domelike portion of the skull that encapsulates the cranial cavity and protects the tissue of the brain. It is comprised of 8 bones that have fused, and are distinguishable by the sutures that have remained at each plate juncture. The frontal, parietal, temporal, and occipital remain the most significant cranial bones, and together form the individual and unique shape of every human skull.

The following page is a frontal and side view of the skull. It shows the placement of all the general highlight and shadows. It also illustrates the skull configuration and the terms associated with it. The location and the way the bones of the face are shaded and highlighted are a direct result of their shape and position. In make-up we have to assume the light source is from above and in front, because the actors are moving around in a three-dimensional world.

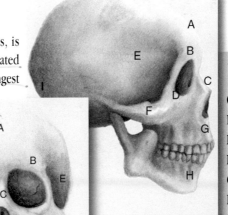

Know
Bone Structure
For Final Exam

A. Frontal Bone
B. SuperciliaryRidge
C. Nasal Bone
D. Malar Bone
E. Temporal Fossa Bone
F. Zygomatic Arch
G. Superior Maxillary Bone
H. Inferior Maxillary Bone
I. Occipital Bone

A. Frontal Bone
B. Superciliary Ridge
C. Nasal Bone
D. Malar Bone
E. Temporal Fossa Bone
F. Zygomatic Arch
G. Superior Maxillary Bone
H. Inferior Maxillary Bone

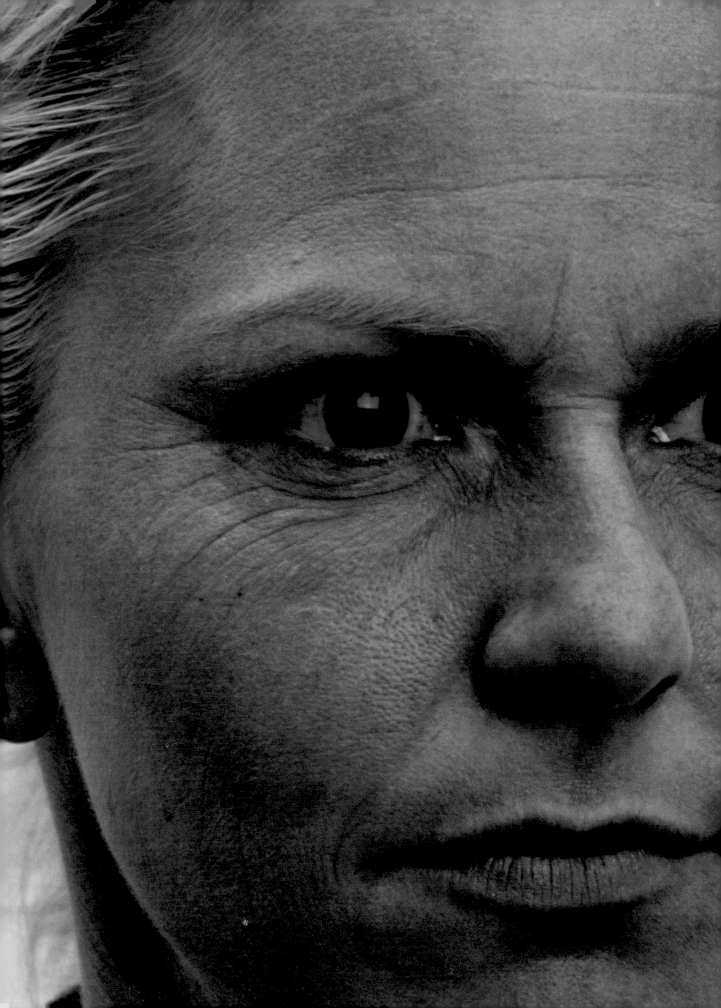

CHAPTER 3

Aging

There are three techniques for aging an actor. The first is a two-dimensional technique with just color or, as we like to call it, highlight and shadow. This section and really the entire book, focuses on the theory of highlight and shadow. This technique is also known as paint and powder make-up and is the process of creating the illusion of age with make-up alone. The second technique, aging stipple, refers to the way latex or sealer is applied. It utilizes latex to create actual three-dimensional wrinkles in the skin as opposed to creating the illusion with color. The third and final technique is the use of prosthetic appliances to create any age. Prosthetic appliances are the most versatile and can be used on just about anyone to create almost any age.

The Process

The following process creates the look of age through the use of color. This is not simply the application of make-up to draw on wrinkles and age spots, but an entire sequence of steps that require a great deal of finesse.

Beginning any make-up application requires the make-up artist to analyze the face. As artists we must first identify the areas of the face we can use and exploit. If the make-up is intended for the theater then the artist will use what the performer has to offer. In addition they will create whatever else may be required in order to get the appropriate age across to the audience. Paint and powder aging techniques used for film and television require a more subtle approach. It is the intent of the artist to achieve realistic detail and age a performer only 10 to 15 years older.

General Highlight & Shadow

We start with the general highlights and shadows, which are those large highlight and shadow areas that show off muscle and bone structure.

Forehead & Temples

The emphasis is on the general highlights and shadows of the forehead and not on the wrinkles. Approach this area by thinking about how foreheads are formed and what shapes are contained within. Male and female skulls are different. First, the male skull is usually larger and has a more prominent brow structure than a female skull; thus the male skull usually has more dips and depressions than a female skull. Start with a shadow and place it in the temple area. It is a depression found just above the cheekbone, behind the eye socket, and below the frontal bone. This depression is turned away from the imaginary light source so it can be fairly dark. While looking at the gray scale this shadow should start out at 8 and blend out to a 5. It should be applied as a soft shadow, blending on both sides and remain darkest at the areas closest to the bones. To see an illustration of the temple area and the bones that make up the area refer to Chapter 2. A soft highlight should be placed on all the high surfaces such as the cheekbone, the eye socket, and the edge of the frontal bone. The lightest spot of the highlight should be closest to the imaginary light source. There is another area of the forehead that must be shadowed; it lies between the brow bone and the round area that makes up the center of the forehead. Now in reality the shadow is being cast by the round area and should be shaded as if a sphere is in the middle of the forehead. Since this shadow is so close to the imaginary light source, which was covered in the sculptural light section, it should start at about #4 and blend out to #2 on the gray scale. Then of course, highlight the very top of the sphere in the middle of the forehead as well as the brow bone. Again, all of the general highlights and shadows of the forehead should be soft.

Eyes

This area of the face could easily go too dark, making the performer look sick. Visualize the eye area and perceive it the way it should look when finished. Take the shadow and apply it along the crease of the eye and be careful not to overdo it. In some situations, allow the crease area to remain untouched. For example, if the model's eyes were already dark, adding more darkness would over exaggerate the effect. Shadow above the lid and emphasize the fatty tissue area. On each person it will be a little different, so shade just enough to create roundness to the bottom of the fatty tissue area. Do not correct the eye area. Next shade under the eye bag area, which will begin to give it more fullness, a great technique is to put a small bit of shading in each corner of the bag and allow the illusion to be created. Do not draw a line of shadow completely under the eye bag. Again, we are not creating wrinkles, so the emphasis is on the general shapes. Using highlight and remembering exactly where our imaginary light source is, apply highlights to the fatty tissue area up close to the eyebrow. The lightest spot of highlight should be the spot closest to the light source. Highlight the bag in the same fashion. The crease needs to be highlighted a little differently; notice the raised area directly below the crease should be a soft highlight that begins to form the top of the nasolabial fold.

Cheekbone

The performer's face structure is what dictates how the cheeks are done. The first one is the gaunt look, shading the structure of the cheekbone up under the eye socket and down into the hollow of the cheek. The second is on a person with a fuller face in which the cheekbone is not well defined. With this type, use shadow to simply depress the area right in front of the ear. The third type is a person with a strong cheekbone. In this case, the shading will follow under the cheekbone and up under the apple of the cheek. In each instance highlight the cheekbone and the other high areas, but remember to create roundness and not an uplifting beauty cheek. Apply the shading in each example as hash marks rather than as a nice, smooth application. This shadow should be broken up and uneven.

With each of these areas we are building onto the next area. As the cheek is applied, identify how it relates to the temple and to the eye area.

Jaw line

There are actually only a couple different ways to do the jaw line. What we are really trying to create is a jowl or two but avoid connecting the corner of the mouth to the jowl, this is a common mistake. Mostly highlight and a very small amount of shadow is applied to create a sphere-like shape along the jawbone. The shadow is applied in a small triangle on the edge of jaw line separating the chin from the rest of the jaw. It is important to remember, every face is unique. Each one may offer differences in terms of some sort of beginning to this jowl and again, tie the jowl into the cheek.

Neck

As with the cheekbone, the weight and facial structure of the performer is going to dictate what style will be used. In most cases just follow the performer's natural features. For example, if the performer's neck is very thin it will show off every muscle, providing a lot of areas to highlight and shadow. If the performer's

neck is really full then all that is needed is a highlight. Remember, more is done with the neck when the wrinkles are added.

Wrinkle Techniques

Since the nasolabial fold is usually the largest wrinkle on the face, it is the best place to illustrate how a wrinkle should be done. Every wrinkle is made up of two highlights and one shadow. The rules of sculptural light still apply to a wrinkle as it would apply to the general highlights and shadows. First, place the shadow into the crease of the fold and blend up and away from the mouth. Apply a sharp edge of the darkest shadow along the edge of the crease. Following the gray scale formula, 10 would be right at the crease and 9 would be just above that then 8 and so on. This shadow would also be considered a hard edge, because one side has a sharp edge and the other side is blended out. As the shadow moves away from the crease it begins to turn towards the light source and starts to turn into a highlight. A sharp edge of highlight is then placed below the crease and blended toward the mouth. This area is a highlight because it is directly exposed to the light source. The last area to contend with is where the shadow turns into a highlight, so as the shadow slowly ends the highlight starts. This highlight is considered a soft highlight, and as it gets closer to the light source it becomes the lightest color. On the gray scale worksheet that color should relate to the value of 1.

All vertical wrinkles are done in this exact same fashion, a sharp edge of shadow right at the crease and blended up then a sharp edge of highlight is applied right below the shadow at the crease and blended down. Finally a soft highlight is applied above the shadow. This is the anatomy of a wrinkle. The application of wrinkles in a stage make-up allows the artist certain liberties; however the artist must follow the facial structure and proper human anatomy. For a film or television make-up the artist only accentuates existing wrinkles intending to exaggerate the effect of age.

The whole trick to creating wrinkles is not to draw them on. Follow the performer's natural features and if they are particularly wrinkle free then create the wrinkles with just highlight. The highlight allows the artist to draw the wrinkles on without it becoming overdone. Remember when using this technique of aging for film and television, the intent is to age the person realistically 10 to 15 years.

Stippling Techniques

The first step is to match the performer's skin color with a base color, then mix a lighter and darker version of that base color. Sounds simple enough but how in the world do we match a performer's skin color? Base matching is an art form that requires a bit of explanation. There are two types of undertone on the planet, one is ruddy or red and the other is a greenish yellow or olive, the olive is the most common and likely to be found. When analyzing the face of the performer, the question of ruddy or olive must be answered. Notice that faces are made up of many colors as opposed to just one color. Observe the color that lies just beneath the surface, not the surface color. We are referring to the color seen in the neck and the color under that surface red. The color will either be greenish-yellow or a light red color. Ninety five percent of the population of the planet is olive while the other 5% is ruddy. We would love to give a simple system of determining which colors to use on an olive person, but unfortunately there is not one. Every manufacturer of base color uses different methods of determining which colors are deemed olive. In addition, a base match might be required in rubber mask grease paints that have no neat system. The best thing to do is take all of the base colors out and simply look at them. This allows the artist to quickly assess which colors are olive and which are ruddy.

After the performer's undertone has been established, the artist evaluates the value of the base match. Quite simply, is the model light or dark? So take the color that best matches their lightness or darkness, their correct undertone, and apply it along the jaw line. This will allow the artist to see how the base color matches the performer's neck. More than likely the color will have to be altered to match perfectly.

In general, color theory is basic and outlines simple rules and guidelines. To take the mystery out of color and make it a completely manageable concept, follow these basic principles. This concept will always be useful in most color situations. The three primary colors are red, blue, and yellow. Every color that can be seen, including base colors are comprised of these three colors. In addition, white is the absence of color and black is an abundance of color. With these five colors we can make anything. For example, to create all of the secondary colors mix two of every combination of primary colors. Red and yellow make orange, yellow and blue make green, and blue and red make purple. If we mix all three primaries together the result will be brown and by adding white will make beige, which is also a base color. By altering how much red or yellow is added to this mixture will change the base color from ruddy to olive. Adding white will lighten and dark brown will darken, which can alter the color further.

Choose a color that is very close to the person's face, then by adding white, brown, red, blue or yellow, it can be altered anyway necessary. Now that the base match of the performer has been determined, mix a small amount of brown into it and create a

darker version. With an orange sponge stipple the darker base color into all the general shadow areas. Use a pair of scissors to round off the sponge before applying the stipple. A rounded sponge will prevent bizarre lines in the make-up application. Allow a small amount of the darker base to be stippled out beyond the shadow areas and into the highlights. Next use the lighter base color, which is created by adding white to the original base color, and stipple it into the highlight area. Again, allow that light color to be stippled out into the shadows. The base match is then stippled over the entire make-up. This will help to even out the colors slightly. Next, apply a small amount of a mustard yellow color over the highlights, it can be mixed with base or just applied carefully. This color should be applied unevenly. Then do the same with a green color. Lastly add a red oxide color, not bright red, to give the skin the required redness. Apply to the end of the nose, to the ears, and to any other area where more warmth is needed. These colors add those necessary shades that give skin the illusion of translucency. They also create a small dotted pattern over the face, with each one helping to create the realistic look of skin.

The make-up artist may choose to powder between each color or apply powder after all the layers of stipple have been applied. However, if the colors begin to mix on the face, powder between each color.

Vein Work

For blue veins use a Teal Professional Pencil and make squiggly lines on the skin. Keep it very light; the idea is that the veins are just beneath the surface of the skin. A brush can also be used, acquiring the make-up from the pencil. Of course, the pencil lines can be softened with a brush. For capillaries use a Red Pencil. If the pencil is hard enough it can be used straight onto the skin. Most of the time the pencil is too soft, so use a small brush to apply the make-up from the pencil to the skin. Use a small amount of 99% alcohol with the brush to get a very thin translucent line. Alcohol-based products offer great vein and capillary colors. However, the consistency of the product should be carefully monitored. If too much alcohol is used, it may run all the other make-up colors together.

Age Spots

Use an eyeliner brush that is smashed down a little. Then stipple a light and medium brown color into the forehead area, creating a light spotted texture. Be very careful, a little goes a long way. The dark color is applied first and then the lighter one is stippled around and on top of the dark one. The idea is to create more texture than actual spots.

Hair-graying Techniques

Hair white is a funny material used for hair-graying. Most manufacturers make it but for the most part it looks just like every other cream make-up on the market. This means the artist can purchase a separate hair white or simply use a cream product that is already in the kit. There are several good liquid hair whites and grays that can be used in combination or alone. Do not use straight white on the hair, as it will look artificial. Use a light yellow on red hair, light orange on black hair and off white on blonde and brown hair. Starting at the base of the hair, brush the color up away from the skin. Do the whole strand of hair, being careful not to get the make-up on the skin. Depending on the desired effect, the make-up artist decides what portions of the character's hair needs color and is usually done after the hairstyle is completed.

Aging Step-By-Step

The following is a photographed complete paint & powder make-up to illustrate how to put all these elements together.

Step 1

Begin with the general shadows. Mix a small amount of the performer's base color to the shadow; about five to ten percent will do. This will give a shadow color that is custom colored for the performer. Do all of the general shadows at one time, starting at the top and working down. The forehead shadows are first then the temple areas. Shadow the eye area then move onto the cheek, the nose, nasolabial folds, and the jaw line. Lastly, shadow the neck.

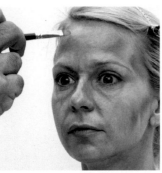

Step 2

Use a large brush or a textured sponge to stipple on the general highlights. Mix about five to ten percent of the performer's base color into the highlight, again creating a custom tint for the highlight. Make the areas closest to the light source the strongest and then use less as the highlight moves closer to the shadow.

Step 3

General highlight and shadow is covered very thoroughly earlier in this chapter. The face becomes very droopy looking with the general highlights and shadows applied.

Step 4

Powder the make-up to set it. Use a powder puff and lightly press the powder into the make-up. Powdering will ensure the make-up for the wrinkles does not mix with the general highlights and shadows.

Step 5

Use the shadow color straight without any base mixed in. This will give the wrinkle shadow a darker look than the general shadows. For the shadow aspect of the wrinkle, paint on a sharp line into the existing crease of the forehead. Blend the color up away from the crease leaving a hard edge on the bottom and a soft blend on top.

Step 6

Use the performer's face as a guide to paint in wrinkle lines wherever a slight or light wrinkle is starting to form. Careful of painting the wrinkles on wherever, aging the performer looks better when you following existing features.

Step 7

The same principle applies to every line; sharp edge on the bottom and a soft edge on top. Lines can be applied around the eyes, in front of the ears, on the neck, and in the corners of the mouth. If the performer is old enough, paint the lines on the lips.

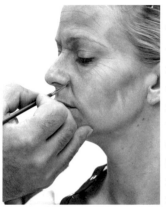

Step 8

The nasolabial fold is also a wrinkle and should be treated in the same way as all the other wrinkles. Note that the nasolabial fold starts behind the nostril and can extend down past the corner of the mouth. However, it should not touch the corner of the mouth.

Step 9

Shadow wrinkles are now added to the performer's face. Again, the shadow parts of the wrinkles are done prior to using any highlight. If doing a theater production more shadow lines can be applied if desired.

Step 10

Highlight is used without mixing in base color. This will allow this highlight to stand out a little more prominently. Like the shadow, start at the top of the face and work down into the neck. Apply a line of highlight color under the shadow wrinkle and then blend it down away from the

color. The highlight line should extend slightly beyond the end of the shadow line. This will help the wrinkle to thin out at the edges.

Step 11

Highlight is added to all the wrinkles, accentuating every wrinkle shadow. It is placed below the shadow, creating a sharp line between each of them; it is then blended downward. A soft highlight is placed above every wrinkle to create the fullness of the wrinkle.

Step 12

Highlight lines can be used alone to create texture. These lines can only be created with highlight and should be kept thin and light. This technique is ideal to create those fine wrinkle lines found around the more pronounced wrinkles. These same lines also help to achieve a sagging fleshy appearance. Apply these types of lines around the eyes, in front of the ears, over the lips, and on the neck.

Step 13

Highlight lines can be applied to the lips, whether or not shadow lines are applied. The lines do a really nice job of defusing the youthful lip line. How old the performer is will dictate how many of these lines are added to the lips.

Step 14

Again, highlight lines are very effective to create wrinkle texture to the neck area. Follow the lines in the neck and make sure to do them lightly and close together. The more lines the better in this case.

Step 15

The finished highlights and shadows as well as all the wrinkles. The make-up at this point looks really severe and a bit heavy. Now add all the flesh tones that will make the performer look more human.

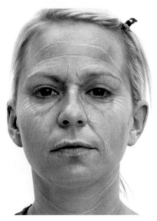

Step 16

Powder all the wrinkles to set them; it will ensure the lines will not mix with the base colors. At this point the performer looks a lot older than a mere ten to fifteen additional years. The next step is going to lessen the look of the aging. It may take a few attempts to achieve a happy medium between how heavy or light to apply the highlights and shadows compared to how heavy the texture is applied.

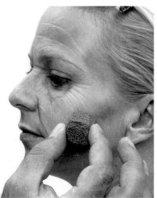

Step 17

Prior to starting this make-up it is important to match the performer's base color to the face. A darker version of that color is stippled into the general shadows; this will soften the shadows and start to blend the overall look.

Step 18

Now mix a lighter version of the performer's base color and stipple it into the highlighted areas. When applying these colors be very careful not to eradicate all the wrinkles and fine lines. The performer's face returns to a more natural color.

Step 19

Use an orange sponge to stipple the base match over the entire face and neck. When creating a make-up of this nature it is very important to always look at it as a complete character and not just as face make-up. That means always make-up the neck and ears.

Step 20

The base colors soften the look or the intensity of the highlights and shadows, creating a textured look that simulates real skin. Powder is used to set the base colors. Lightly powder the make-up using a colorless powder, powdering between the layers of make-up creates a transparent look.

Step 21

Various colors such as green, yellow, and red are mixed with the base match and stippled into areas of the face. Look at real pictures of old people to see where some of these colors are placed. These colors will help create translucency to the make-up, even when in reality it can be thick or opaque.

Green works best on men for beard shadow, however it can also be used on female performers, the trick is to apply it in a few areas. The same applies for the yellow or mustard color. A brick red color can be used straight or mixed with bases, apply it to the end of the nose and to the cheeks.

Step 23

A teal color is used to create veins. Veins are not necessarily an effect of old age but they do help to add realism to the make-up by adding translucency. Use a really light touch to create a soft blueness. Apply the veins to the temple area, the neck and the under eye area.

Step 24

Capillaries are used to show aging since the older we get the more likely they are to appear. They can also be used to show character traits such as a heavy drinker. The capillaries are applied with a brush. Rub a dark red make-up onto the palette and then dip the brush into 99% alcohol. Lightly apply small and thin squiggly lines to the face. Capillaries can be applied anywhere; ears, cheeks, and the nose can receive a higher concentration of them.

Step 25

A small amount of translucent powder is used to set the whole make-up and to complete the look.

When doing aging make-up, remember we are aging the performer believably and not painting them old; the after photograph is sagging more than the before and it appears as if gravity is starting to pull down on the skin.

Overlay Drawing

Before opening the make-up case or touching a brush to an actor's face, there should be a well thought out plan for the make-up. An overlay drawing is the way a make-up artist visualizes a character two dimensionally. This applies even in a situation that only requires the actress to look more beautiful. Whether creating an eye treatment for a beauty make-up or an elaborate aging make-up, overlay drawings will allow the artist to design and plan out every aspect of a make-up.

There are two different ways of creating this type of drawing for a production. The first is to use tracing paper over a picture of the actor and draw the make-up design using the actor's face as a guide. The other way is to scan the actor's photograph into a computer and use a program like Adobe PhotoShop to design the make-up on the digital version of the photograph.

There are two reasons to do a make-up design; producers and production personnel need a clear-cut idea of what the make-up will look like and other artists will be able to use the design as a guide during the actual make-up application.

Start with an 8" x 10" photograph of the actor (usually provided by the production company), professional colored pencils, and a pad of tracing paper. The design in the example is of an aging make-up. Do not worry about which type of make-up or technique will be used to actually age the actor. This is the design phase that will illustrate what the actor should look like in her eighties and enable the production company to see how she will look in their film.

Tape the photograph down completely to a tabletop or to a clipboard. Lay a piece of tracing paper or velum over the photograph and tape along the top edge. Allow the bottom of the piece of tracing paper to remain unattached, so a sheet of white paper can be inserted underneath it. This will allow the artist to check the progress of the drawing.

The pencils used in this example are Prismacolor Artist's Pencils, but any professional brand of pencil will work. Use the color Burnt Ochre to begin to trace the face. Outline the general features and the areas that are in a fixed position or the areas that are not going to change as a result of the design. In this case the eyes, nostrils, edge of the face, clothes and general shadows that are present in the photograph will be incorporated into the finished design. Slide a white sheet of paper underneath the tracing paper and above the actual photograph. The paper separates the drawing from the photograph and allows the drawing to be viewed on its own. The artist then can make changes and additions to the basic structure of the face. Check progress often by inserting the white paper.

Use the side of the Burnt Ochre pencil to softly draw in the shadows that create all of the general shadows of the face. Next add age lines along with other small details. Create sharp edges of shadow in each crease or wrinkle and blend upward. Pressing harder on the pencil and going over the same area repeatedly will make those areas darker. This technique allows the artist to create shape and dimension.

The Dark Umber pencil will add depth to dark areas, such as the nostrils, eyes, and the general shadows. Sharpen the wrinkle lines and deepen the shadows with it as well. Use the Beige pencil to add a nice even tone to the whole drawing and begin to soften the shadows. The preliminary highlights are added with the Cream pencil or by lightly applying the Beige over the highlights. The drawing will look a bit yellow because of the Beige and will need to be warmed up.

Use the Peach pencil to add a subtle redness to the shadow areas and into the wrinkles. The Light Peach pencil is used as a highlight and added to the general highlight areas. This color will add additional warmth and can be used to blend or soften any hard edges. The drawing may need additional refinement depending on what is needed. Some of the lines and wrinkles may need to be darkened as the drawing progresses.

Detail colors are added at this point. A bit of green may be added to the overall skin tone to give it a more olive look. The actor's hair may need to be changed to match their older age. Use Black or Dark Brown as the main shadow for the hair and Gray as a highlight. Gray can also be used in the shadows to increase depth. The eyes should be colored the same as the actor's; Black is used around the pupil and in the lashes. Peach can be used on the cheek, chin, nose and forehead to add subtle warmth. Complete the details by adding capillaries to the nose, chin and cheeks. Use Terra Cotta to add red into the fleshy area of the eyes and subtle redness to the skin. To create age spots and veins on the forehead and cheeks, use Light Umber and Teal. Use of the White pencil and Light Peach can soften some of the colors and are very useful when blending colors together. As with any drawing the artist is going to choose which colors are needed and depending on the finished design the colors may vary.

The artist has the choice to present the finished drawing with the original picture underneath it or side by side with the original drawing. Either way will allow the production staff to see exactly what the artist is intending to do with the make-up. The finished drawing should first and foremost look like the performer. Secondly, it should be aged to the desired age range. Based on the drawing, the production company will have a clear understanding of what the actor will look like in the make-up.

The following is a photographic step-by-step of how an overlay drawing is done.

Step 1

Use an 8"x10" photograph. For the purpose of learning the process use a photo of yourself, someone famous, or possibly a friend.

Step 2

Outline the shape of the face and its key areas, including the general shadows.

Step 3

Darken the general shadows and create the new structure of the face.

Step 4

Add the wrinkles and create warmth with peach.

Step 5

Use a darker color to add depth to the shadows and wrinkles.

Step 6

Warm up the shadows with Peach and use Light Peach as a highlight and to soften some of the hard edges.

Step 7

Add detail colors into the drawing.

Step 8

Black is used as the main shadow for the hair and gray as an accent. The hairstyle is changed to match the make-up.

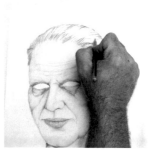

Step 9

Warmth is added to the cheek, chin, nose, and forehead. Gray, Black, and Dark Brown are added into the hair and eyes, as well as lashes.

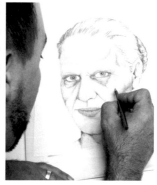

Brown is used to darken and to soften some of the shadows.

Capillaries are added to the nose, chin, and cheeks. Red is added into the eyes. Veins and age spots are added to the forehead and cheeks.

Aging Stipple

Aging stipple is a technique of applying a make-up material. It is used to create superficial lines and wrinkles. The application of aging stipple is used as a three-dimensional make-up medium. Latex and similar products, such as Duo Eyelash Adhesive are the most traditional stipple mediums, although today there are a variety of proprietary aging stipple products. Vinyl or plastic concentrates and fixatives offer today's make-up artist a latex-free alternative when using an aging stipple product.

Latex-based stipple mediums are very reliable products; however latex will absorb the vehicle in regular types of make-up, causing the make-up to discolor on the surface of the latex. This requires the make-up artist to use rubber mask grease paint to color the product.

For the most part, latex-based stipple products will create a fairly strong durable make-up, but it may become necessary to increase the bond between the skin and the stipple product. Areas of extreme movement, like the area around the mouth, may require a preliminary layer of Pros-aide adhesive. It is important to note the more layers of latex you use, the more wrinkles you will create. Be careful, too many layers of latex will create a monster.

The age stipple technique was first used in the original "Mummy" film to make the actor appear really old. Since then it has been used on numerous films to create a variety of ages. The most notable examples were on Jessica Tandy in "Driving Miss Daisy" and on Gloria Stuart in "Titanic." Both films were nominated for an Academy Award for Make-up and one of them won. The other similarity between these two films are that both actresses were in their eighties; the point is, this technique works very well in creating wrinkles on older skin. Therefore, this technique is useful if the performer is older, has very pliable skin and the desired target age includes wrinkles.

If you are trying to age someone to fifty using only age stipple, this technique is not the best choice. It may however be used to create a specific look or as the basis of several other character effects.

The process of applying age stipple to the entire face requires the artist to work in specific sections of the neck and face, and layer the application upwards. If the artist determines that only certain areas of the face are necessary to apply age stipple, there is no specific order required.

Working on the neck requires the performer to look up as the artist pulls down on his chest. This will create horizontal wrinkles on the neck as well as the jaw line and back to the ear. The performer then places a hand on his ear, and the artist places a hand upon the performer's chin stretching the skin horizontally; this creates vertical wrinkles over the cheek. The rest of the cheek and the nasolabial fold area should follow. The performer should pull his mouth down and away from the nasolabial fold while the artist pulls up and out on the cheek bone. The lips and chin require the artist to place a finger on each side of the performer's mouth, and stretch apart.

The eyes should be done in three parts. First, create the crows' feet at the outer corners of the eyes by pulling down on the performer's cheek and up on the temple area. To apply age stipple to the upper lid, the performer should hold his lashes down while the artist lifts up on the eyebrows. The under-eye area is the trickiest; the performer should pull his nose down and away from the eye as the artist pulls down on the cheek. Pull down and away on the outside cheek area. Applying age stipple to the forehead will require the artist to pull down on the eyebrows and hold the hairline in place.

It is rare that an artist will choose to apply age stipple to the entire face. This is a time-consuming process which only creates one type of effect. Ideally only small areas in conjunction with a prosthetic appliance or paint and powder make-up are applied. In "Titanic," the make-up on Gloria Stuart was very subtle; a combination of highlight, shadow, and aging stipple was used to believably age her to one hundred and one.

It should be stressed that the age stipple technique requires the artist to follow this specific order. It is important to note, the direction in which the skin is stretched will directly affect the shape and flow of the wrinkles formed on the skin. The artist can create horizontal wrinkles by stretching the skin vertically and vertical wrinkles by stretching the skin horizontally.

The most common use of age stipple incorporates the use of a paint and powder make-up and aging stipple applied in the eye area. Coloring this make-up must be done with rubber mask grease paint because latex is a rubber. However, translucent washes of color are recommended as opposed to opaque applications. The latex is naturally translucent and it is possible to blend by using a small amount of K-Y Jelly. The most effective use of this effect, will age a performer by accentuating natural wrinkles, but will require the face of a mature performer.

Five Rules

There are five very simple rules that must be followed exactly or the technique will not work:

1 *Stretch the skin*
2 *Apply the latex*
3 *Dry the latex*
4 *Powder the latex*
5 *Release the skin*

Step 1

The models skin should be cleaned before applying an aging stipple. In this example we will apply liquid latex around the eye to age that area.

Step 2

The skin at the outside of the eye is stretched and latex is applied to create horizontal wrinkles. Latex is a contact adhesive. If the latex dries on the sponge and on the skin, touching the two surfaces together will cause the sponge to adhere to the model's face.

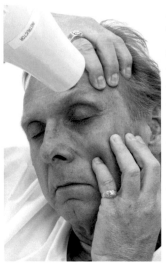

Step 3

Two thin layers of latex are applied to the area. Several thin layers of latex are better than one thick layer. Keep the edges thin and blended into the skin. Use a blow-dryer to completely dry the latex. Continue to hold the skin in position as you dry the latex. (Make sure that your blow dryer is set to a low heat so that you do not burn the performer.)

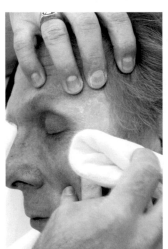

Step 4

Apply powder over the dried latex with a powder puff. This will keep the latex from sticking to itself. Release the skin only after the latex has been stippled.

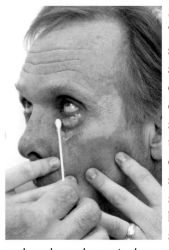

Step 5

The model is helping by stretching the lower eye lid area. The lower eye is pulled down in three different directions. We are trying to achieve a curved wrinkle under the eye, so we pull down across the nose, straight down from the eye, and down across the cheek bone. Two layers of latex are applied to the area; a cotton swab can be used to get in close to the lower lashes.

Step 6

For the larger area under the eye, we suggest using a sponge. Be careful of any dry areas of latex, and make sure you are blending the overlapping areas of latex. Do not leave space between each area of latex.

Step 7

Dry the latex then apply powder. The performer can now open his eye without it sticking open.

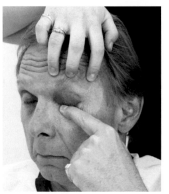

Step 8

Stretch the upper eyelid area and apply latex. The model is helping to hold the lid down as the eyebrow is pulled up. A cotton swab may work better to get in close to the performers lashes.

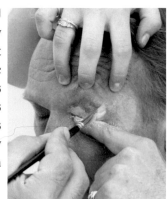

Step 9

Apply powder. You may need to use a brush to get the powder close to the lashes. The eyelid area is very thin. Use caution as you apply the powder. It is very easy to accidentally stick the skin together in this area.

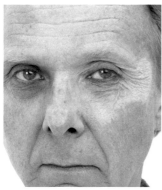

The eye area is completely powdered and ready to be colored. Remove the excess powder using a small amount of K-Y Jelly or any other water-soluble lubricant. The advantage to using a water soluble material, as opposed to using oil, is the artist can lessen the amount of material used with water.

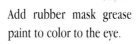

Add rubber mask grease paint to color to the eye.

The complete effect on the left eye illustrates how to incorporate an aging stipple effect with a paint and powder make-up application.

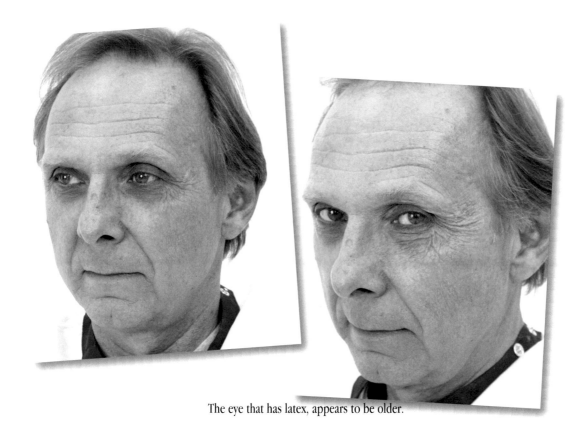

The eye that has latex, appears to be older.

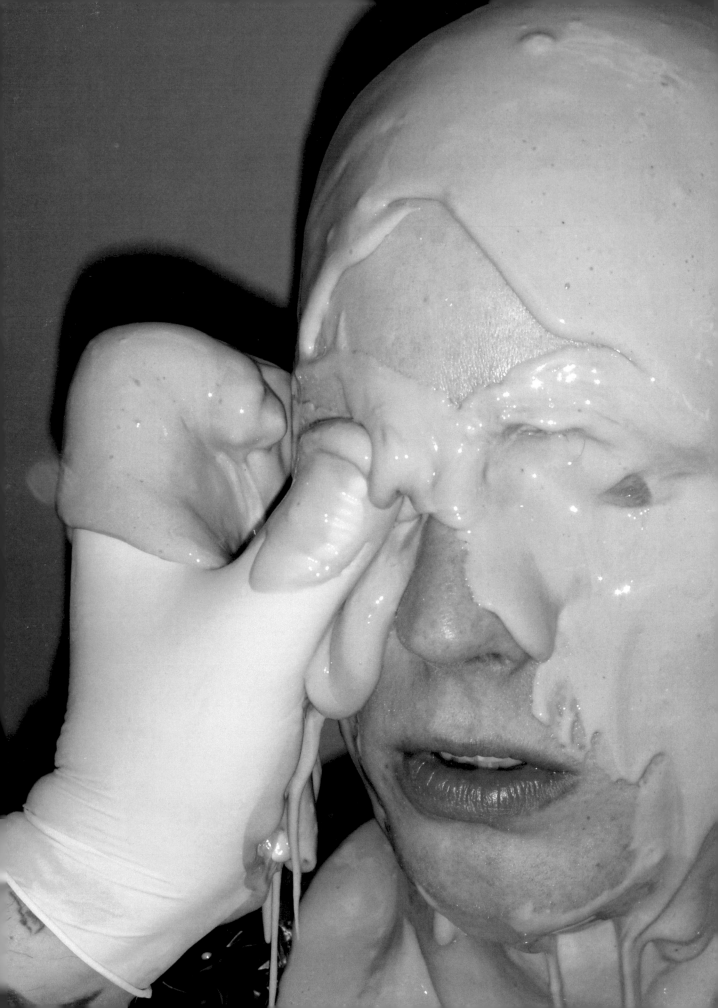

CHAPTER 4

Prosthetic Appliances

In the following chapters we will focus on how to make prosthetic appliances, from taking a life cast to using a variety of materials for the appliances themselves. This is an introduction to prosthetic appliances and their use. We could write an entire book on this subject, but instead will give a comprehensive look at how prosthetics are made and applied as well as the different types of materials available today.

Introduction To Prosthetics

Foam latex has been the staple material for prosthctic appliances since its first use. In recent years there has been a push for more realistic materials, such as gelatin and silicone. However, several artists continue to use foam with stunning success. Before we explain how to apply a prosthetic, we should first talk about how it is made. Production tends to believe that prosthetics magically appear on set. It is our responsibility, the make-up artist, to educate production as to what it required to produce a prosthetic appliance. It is very important for a make-up artist to understand and be able to explain the process to production.

With so many choices out there, how do we decide which material is best? Each material has advantages and disadvantages. There are several: latex, foam latex, gelatin, silicone GFA (gel filled appliances), foamed gelatin, polyurethane foam, and Pros-Aide transfer appliances.

Latex is used primarily in the Halloween industry and sometimes on stage. It is poured into a mold and allowed to dry. Latex appliances are very simple to make and are extremely durable, however, latex does not move well and may be hard to blend into the surrounding skin.

Foam latex is the most common material used today. It is light, soft, extremely flexible, and compresses well. It is completely opaque, meaning light and color cannot pass through it. This type of appliance is best suited for make-ups where it is unnecessary for a performer's skin tone to show through. It is also the best choice for large or thick prosthetic appliances especially if an artist creates a green monster and translucency will not be an issue. Foam latex prosthetic appliances are one of the most durable materials.

Gelatin is used mainly for small appliances such as injuries. It is translucent and flexible, however it does not compress well. Its translucency is its greatest asset, and it is very easy to apply and color. Another nice feature of gelatin is that the edges can be dissolved with witch hazel. For small applications, under the right conditions it is an ideal appliance material.

Silicone GFA is one of the most realistic feeling prosthetic appliances. It is silicone gel covered with an encapsulator. The top of the appliance, or the outer skin of it, moves independently of the skin attached to the actor's face. This gives the appliance very believable movement; it is also a very translucent appliance and seems to work best when thin. Some artists have stated they prefer to apply silicone GFA as one piece, as opposed to doing a multi-piece prosthetic make-up. We have found that applying one piece is faster; however, working with multiple pieces is no different than working in any other material.

Foam gelatin is very similar to gelatin appliances. It is translucent but not as much as regular gelatin. The big difference between the two is movement; foam gelatin compresses well so it moves better. Due to the weight of the gelatin this type of prosthetic is best used thin.

Polyurethane appliances are mostly used in Europe for stage productions, and rarely used on film due to their lack of movement; they are best used for an area with little or no movement, like a bone protruding from a leg or a nose. The softest polyurethane foam is still harder than foam latex. An experienced artist can of course make any material look good.

Pros-Aide Transfer appliances are translucent, durable appliances that stretch and compress with the movement of the skin. Transfer appliances are colored intrinsically, tinted to resemble a realistic skin tones. These appliances are typically used to simulate injuries or smaller prosthetic appliances.

Prosthetic make-up is a very diverse subject. In this book we are not trying to educate the artist on every aspect of making a prosthetic appliance, rather our focus is on the application of them. A general overview is provided to give a make-up artist the basic understanding about this subject, and help them speak intelligently to production regarding the many aspects of prosthetic construction and application. It is a step-by-step look at what it takes to make an appliance for a project.

Making a prosthetic appliance is usually done the same way regardless of the materials being used. First, a life cast is done of the performer and then a sculpture in oil-based clay is made of the desired piece. A negative mold is then made of the sculpture and the clay is removed from the molds and thoroughly cleaned. An appliance material is used to fill the space in the molds left by the clay. The mold is opened, and a prosthetic appliance is removed. The prosthetic appliance is designed to custom fit the model of the original life cast.

Although that was an overly simplified description of how to make a prosthetic appliance, it is easy to see why a custom piece of this nature can be very expensive. Once the molds are made, many pieces can be produced from them, enabling us to maintain the continuity of the make-up each time it is applied, particularly as each piece can only be used once. The following chapters will cover more thoroughly the making of different prosthetic appliances, as well as how they are applied.

The following is a step-by-step procedure on how to create a prosthetic appliance.

Life Casting With Alginate

Life casting is the process of taking an impression of a live model, using materials that are now standard in the special make-up effects industry. The most common impression material is alginate, sometimes referred to as P.G.C. or prosthetic grade cream. Alginate is often used to replicate areas of the body, such as the human head or face, and can be used over large portions of the body to replicate arms and legs, and sometimes a model's entire body.

Alginate ranges in brand and color, with each specific manufacturer attributing specific qualities and abilities to their product. No specific alginate has been found to be "the best" as a standard in this industry, in fact, many lab technicians and make-up effects artists have their own opinion on which alginate material is superior to others. Always perform a mix test with any unfamiliar alginate. Before proceeding with a life cast, refer to the manufacturer's recommendations or directions.

Alginate is a temperature sensitive material, and once applied to the model it may have an acceler-ated set time, dependant upon several conditions. The high temperature of the room, the model, the water in the mixture, or mixing long and vigorously may all contribute to a rapid set time. Cooler tempera-tures will increase

the working time, and water temperatures are often adjusted to achieve desired results.

The performer is prepared for a life cast of the face or head by combing back the hair and fitting a bald cap. A bald cap is used to protect the performer's hair and prevent the alginate or other impression material from tangling into the hair. The perimeter of the hairline is demarcated with an indelible copy pencil, essentially a water transferable ink pencil that cannot be erased. The Sanford NoBlot copy pencil packaged as a "bottle of ink in a pencil" is commonly available online or may be purchased at a local art supply retail store. This line will be transferred onto the alginate and then onto your positive mold. The line will indicate to the sculptor exactly where the hairline is located.

In some cases, the bald cap can stick to the alginate or impression material. This may pose a potential problem, resulting in a torn or ruined life cast. A light coat of castor oil can be applied to the surface of the bald cap, and will help to release the alginate when the life cast is removed. Do not apply castor oil over the copy pencil lines; it will prevent the lines from transferring onto the alginate life cast. All facial or body hair, like eyelashes, eyebrows, or chest hair visible in the life cast area should be coated with petroleum jelly to keep them from being pulled when you remove the life cast.

The alginate impression material and water are measured into two separate bowls. The type of alginate and temperature of water used will affect the working time of the impression material. Setting time may be adjusted, by changing the temperature of the water, or by adding an alginate retarder. Setting time refers to the time an artist has to work and apply the material, before it "sets", becoming firm and unworkable. Prosthetic grade creams may offer an extended working time when using cooler water, and may be accelerated when supplementing a warmer temperature of water. Dental grade alginates, designed to set quickly, are best used when duplicating small specific areas of the face, or when creating teeth and mouth castings.

Most prosthetic grade creams will offer the artist about 7 minutes of working time. It is advisable to perform a test with all alginates prior to the life cast application and confirm the set time and workability. Mix the material according to the manufacturer's recommendations, and make any necessary adjustments based upon a batch test. Pour the water into the alginate while slowly stirring by hand to incorporate the impression powder. Continue to stir until achieving a smooth creamy consistency, making sure there are no chunks of unmixed alginate.

Begin with the performer sitting in an upright position. The bowl of alginate should be easily accessible, perhaps ask the performer to hold the bowl in their lap for convenience. Gently spread the alginate, starting at the top of the head, making sure the alginate is going on smoothly and evenly. Work the alginate down each side of the performer's face, using large sweeping motions. Apply generous amounts to cover the impression area, avoid thin spots and achieve an estimated thickness of one-quarter inch. The artist can prevent air pockets from forming against the skin by gently massaging a small amount of alginate into deep formations of the face like the recessions at the corners of the mouth and eyes, and the curvature of the wings of the nostril.

Alginate is carefully applied to the bridge of the nose, nostrils, and septum area, always leaving the nostril opening clear of material so that the model can easily breathe. The nose area and breathing passages should be closely monitored during the life cast process in order to avoid any potential obstructions. Once everything is covered allow the alginate to completely set up.

When the alginate is set, all surface detail is replicated, but the alginate will remain flexible. Plas-ter bandages must be applied over the alginate, creating a mother mold, cradling and supporting the true shape of the alginate impression.

A plaster bandage is a cotton bandage infused with a prepared plaster that will harden after it has been saturated with water. Plaster bandages are most commonly associated with orthopedic casts used to encapsulate a limb, holding a broken bone in place.

Prepare the plaster bandages by tearing them into two different lengths, with one pile large and the other small. The specific size is based on that of the cast as well as what the artist may be used to working with. An average life cast of the face will usually require about four rolls of six-inch plaster bandages. Prepare a bowl with hot water and place near the performer. The warmer the water the faster the plaster bandages will set. Specialty plaster bandages available are designed to harden within very specific set times, and packaged as regular, fast, and extra fast set.

Plaster bandages of the same length are dipped into the water, wringing out the excess and applied to the surface of the alginate. The bandages may be applied as individual strips, or in stacks of up to three. By applying three layers at a time the artist will be able to build up a good strong thickness from the beginning.

Make-up artists have differing opinions and preferences as to where to begin the bandage application. Some artists prefer to begin at the outside and work towards the center, while others begin at the center and finish with the perimeter. In all circumstances the objective is clear and specific. Bandages are layered and overlapped to create a strong framework or supportive shell. This is designed to hold the impression material in the intended position. While applying bandages on the life cast of the face, carefully contour them to the shapes of the face and the surface of the alginate. Cover the entire face area and do not obstruct the breathing passages. Each layer will overlap the previous layer; the entire cast should be about six layers thick.

Removing the life cast will require the performer to flex their facial muscles, making expressions and slowly exhaling through the mouth. These movements and the air exhaled will release the suction holding the alginate to the performer's face. Grip each side of the cast and gently pull, slowly working it off the face. Be careful, the cast may stick slightly to the bald cap or any exposed hair, so go slow.

Once completed, the life casting process creates an impression mold, often referred to as a negative. This must be filled with a casting material to create a positive, or a duplicate of the form in fully realized three dimensions.

Step 1

Apply a bald cap to protect the performer's hair, and a plastic drape to protect the clothing. Use a copy pencil to mark the hairline. Apply castor oil to the bald cap. Apply petroleum jelly to eyebrows and eyelashes, and all exposed hair.

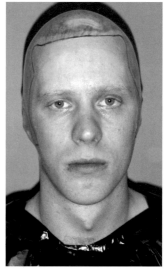

Step 2

Pour water slowly into the alginate. Stir and mix the alginate until it achieves a creamy consistency.

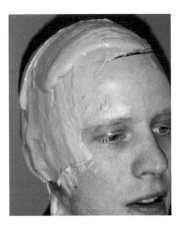

Step 3

Carefully spread the alginate over the top of the head, making sure it is going on smooth and evenly.

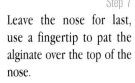

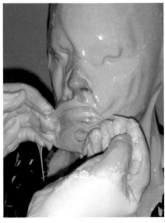

Step 7

Leave the nose for last, use a fingertip to pat the alginate over the top of the nose.

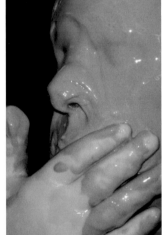

Step 4

Work the alginate down each side of the performer's face, using large sweeping motions. Use handfuls of alginate to do each side and remember not to apply it too thin.

Step 8

Monitor the nose area. Do not allow the alginate to obstruct the breathing passages. There is no need for any straws

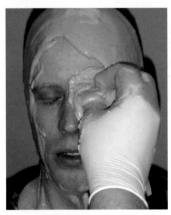

Step 5

Gently massage the alginate into the corners of each eye placing the alginate into the eye area in this fashion will help alleviate any air bubbles in the corners of the eyes. Cover each eye with the alginate

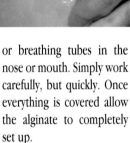

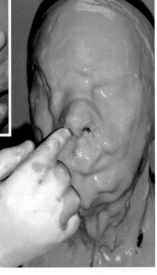

or breathing tubes in the nose or mouth. Simply work carefully, but quickly. Once everything is covered allow the alginate to completely set up.

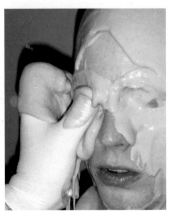

Step 6

Gently massage the alginate into the corners of the mouth and across the lip line. Cover the mouth area with alginate.

Step 9

Prepare the plaster bandages by tearing them into two different lengths, with one pile large and the other small. An average life cast of the face will usually require about four rolls of six-inch plaster bandages. Prepare a bowl with hot water and place near the performer.

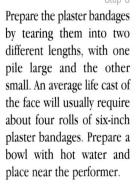

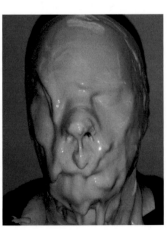

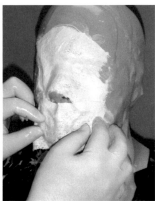

Step 10
Starting at the center, single bandages are applied to the nose and face to precisely fit the intricate contours of this crucial area.

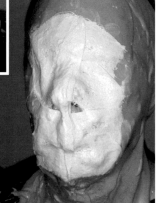

Step 13
Cover the entire face area with horizontal and vertical stacks of plaster bandages. This creates a mother mold at a uniform six layers thick. Place bandages to carefully contour to the shapes of the nose and face. Do not obstruct the breathing passages.

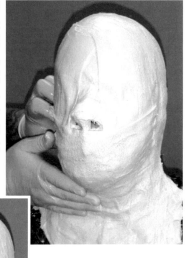

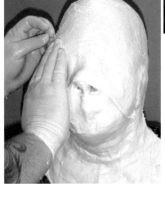

Step 11
Using three bandages of the same length a defined perimeter is established, starting at the top of the head and dividing down the center.

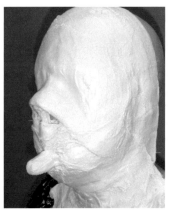

Step 14
Plaster bandages have been gathered and shaped to simulate a stilt. Placing stilts on the chin and forehead will allow the artist to rest the life cast down. This avoids any deformation that may occur when a life cast rests upon the features of the face.

Step 15
The forehead stilts have been placed. Let the cast cure for about five minutes or until it is hard to the touch. Do not knock on the cast. Take this opportunity to clean up some of the materials and the performer.

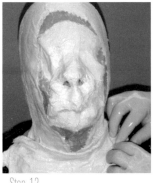

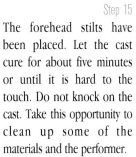

Step 12
Complete the perimeter framework of the bandage application by applying a stack of three bandages at the base of the neck. Layer the stacks horizontally and vertically, overlapping each prior piece.

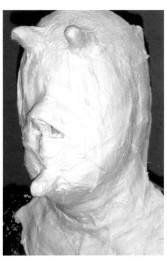

Removing the life cast will require the performer to flex facial muscles, making expressions and slowly exhaling through the mouth. Grip each side of the cast and gently pull, slowly working it off the face.

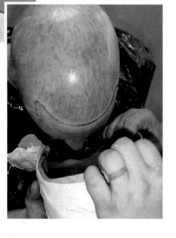

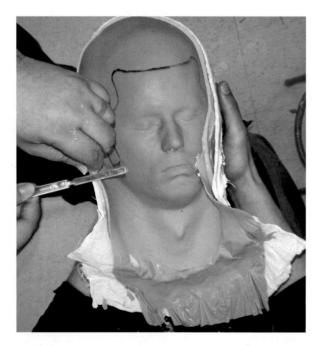

Step 17

The finished cast in alginate is now ready to be filled. Notice the cast appears to be a positive image of the performer, but in reality it is a negative impression of the face.

The Positive Mold

A positive mold is a duplicate of the performer's face used to model a sculpture and become the core element of a prosthetic mold. The impression of the performer, made by the alginate and supported in a plaster bandage mother mold, must be filled with a casting material to create a positive mold.

The casting material may be specific urethanes, not affected by the residual moisture content of the alginate, such as BJB TC-1630, or a project specific gypsum-based stone. Ultracal-30 is commonly used to create positives, and will later be used in conjunction with a mold negative, to bake and produce foam latex appliances. White Hydrocal is often used to create positives, which can be used as reference, or used as a first generation "master" to produce countless molds without inconveniencing the performer. In most European countries, the previously mentioned gypsum stones are often difficult to locate, and dental grade stones are generally substituted.

This positive mold will be an exact copy of the actor duplicated in cement-like stone called Ultracal-30. This positive mold is created directly from the life cast of the performer. The alginate cast needs to be filled upon its removal from the performer or it will shrink, defeating the purpose of casting the actor in the first place. Reinforcement material is essential to creating a strong mold that will last a long time. Either hemp or burlap cut into strips can be used for reinforcing this mold.

Step 1

Fill a large bowl one third full of warm water, slowly sifting in small amounts of Ultracal-30. Coat the surface then allow the cement

to sink. Sprinkle in more cement until the material stops sinking. It will be apparent enough cement is added to the water because it will form a dried lakebed appearance in the bowl. Allow to stand for a moment and then mix together. A Jiffy Mixer can be used, but beware, it will cause the cement to set up faster. In most cases a hand will work best to thoroughly mix the cement.

Step 2

Use a small brush to carefully paint in the Ultracal-30 over the entire surface of the alginate. This first layer is called the splash coat; its name comes from an old technique in which the artist used to splash the cement into a mold or over a sculpture. Be very careful not to trap air bubbles in the cement as it is painted over the alginate.

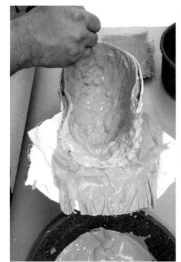

Step 3

As the Ultracal-30 thickens, continue to build the thickness to about half an inch. Work slowly making sure the cement is a uniform thickness. The vertical surfaces are the hardest area to build up. Slowly scoop cement from the bottom of the mold and move it to the sides. Repeat this step until the cement stops sliding down. Allow this first layer to set but not cure.

Step 4

Once the first layer is set, mix up another batch of Ultracal-30. This batch is for the reinforcement layer. Either burlap cut into strips or hemp balled up into a nest can be utilized. Dip the hemp or the burlap into the bucket of cement and wring out the excess cement. Apply the soaked fibers all over the surface of the mold. Add a second layer of fibers around the edge of the mold to strengthen it.

Step 5

A wooden handle can be inserted into the mold at this point. Wrap the ends of the handle with burlap or hemp for added strength.

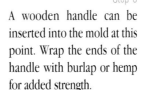

Step 6

Mix a third and final batch of Ultracal-30. This batch will be the beauty coat. Just as the name implies, this will make the mold pretty. Mix up this batch a little thicker than the previous batches. Apply it with a spatula, a kidney tool, or fingers. Fill in all low areas and flatten any sharp areas.

Step 7

Use a small amount of water on a sponge or a rubber kidney tool. Smooth out the surface, as the cement cures it will heat up and quickly become un-workable—so work fast.

Step 8

Allow the Ultracal-30 to completely cure and then pull the positive cast out of the alginate negative mold. The cast is now ready to be cleaned. The alginate mold should be discarded. If this life cast negative is made of a silicone impression material then the mold can be saved and other casts produced from it.

The positive cast needs to be cleaned of all sharp edges, air bubbles, and any other imperfections. Use a sharp tool and carefully knock off any raised areas. A hand planer can be used to round off the edges and smooth out the corners of the cast. If necessary, mix up a small amount of Ultracal-30 to repair any holes in the positive.

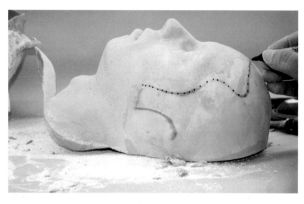

Step 10

As soon the positive cast is clean, remark the hairline. Apply a coat of castor oil over the positive surface. This will condition it and help the surface of the cast to last longer. As the Ultracal-30 continues to dry out and lose moisture, the castor oil will replace that moisture, and not affect the foam latex that will be run in it later.

Sculpting Prosthetics

Prosthetic sculpture is the art of modeling clay onto a positive form. Often working on a life cast positive, the sculptor will create and manipulate the forms of the face. They will replicate an intended look that is based on a rendering, compiled from reference, or straight from the artist's imagination. Prosthetic sculpture requires an artist to have knowledge of general anatomy and understand how sculpture thickness relates to prosthetic movements.

The look of a character can be modeled using many varieties of oil-based clays. Roma Plastalina is typically used to sculpt prosthetic appliances. However, some materials such as silicone have an adverse reaction to the sulfur in the clay. Chavant NSP clay is becoming a popular choice for sulfur-free clay, as it seems to be more consistent in texture and density than the Roma Plastalina.

Sculpting a prosthetic is a process that begins with "blocking" or "roughing out" the sculpture. This is a term that is used to describe the process of assertively placing small pieces of clay, pressed and positioned on the positive to represent large forms and general anatomical structures of the face that the sculptor wants to manipulate or reshape.

The rough out requires the sculptor to arrange these forms so that they may be incorporated believably into the anatomy of the performer. Essentially, the rough out of the sculpture allows an artist to sketch and realize a characters' form in the third dimension.

When dramatically altering a characters appearance with a facial prosthetic, the sculptor must regularly evaluate the balance and symmetry of the sculpture. As this relates to facial prosthetics it means an artist understands how certain elements relate to each other on the sculpture and on the face. A balanced and symmetrical facial sculpture will appear to be equal in weight, mass, shape, and sizing of anatomical structures such as the forehead, temples, cheeks, jaw line, general wrinkles and folds.

Although it is true that few things in nature are perfectly balanced and symmetrical, theses key sculptural features should not be grossly disproportionate, obvious, or distracting to the casual observer, unless that is the intended look. A defect, malformation, or mutation for example, might intentionally be imbalanced and asymmetrical.

With the rough out complete, smaller sculptural forms are refined. The folds and wrinkles of the character's skin are developed and finessed. Texture is applied with a variety of sponges, stamps, and tools, and softened with solvents such as acetone and alcohol to appear organic and natural. The completed prosthetic sculpture is protected with a plastic sealer or spray. Krylon Crystal Clear or Glatzan, thinned with acetone, will each provide adequate protection of the final textures.

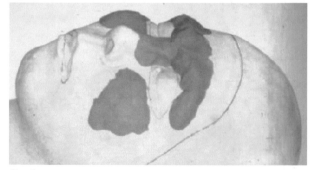

Step 1

The first step to sculpting a prosthetic appliance is to rough out the sculpture. Do this by applying small pieces of softened clay to the surface of the cast. The cast represents the performer's face with small pieces of clay applied to alter the features. Do not worry about detail at this point. Simply build up a rough version of the sculpture.

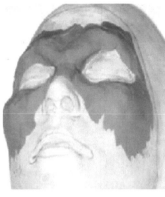

Step 2

Focus on symmetry and getting the proper look of the character. Blend the small pieces together only to make sure there are no gaps in the clay. At this point, the focus is not to smooth the whole thing out.

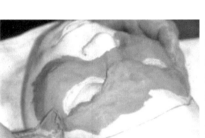

Step 3

Once the sculpture is the proper shape it is ready to be refined. Using different sizes of rakes begin to smooth down the clay. The rake is a sculpting tool with many small teeth. Use the largest rake first, working down to a very fine rake. The teeth of the rake drag across the clay removing the high spots and filling the low spots (crisscrossing this tool really starts to smooth out the sculpture). Raking over the edge of the clay helps to create a fine blended edge, but be careful not to scratch the surface of the cast.

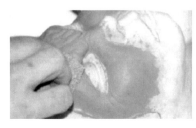

Step 4

Now that the shape is really taking form, start to create wrinkles and texture. Carve in the heavy wrinkles first and then the smaller ones; each time use a couple of rakes to smooth out the wrinkles, giving them realistic roundness. Small bits of clay can be added here and there to create veins and also to add fullness or roundness to an area. A rubber tool can be used to blend and taper the delicate edges of the sculpture. A small amount of 99% alcohol or acetone can also be used to smooth out the wrinkles and the skin textures.

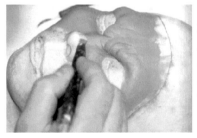

Step 5

Texture the whole sculpture with a small sponge or a texture pad. Be careful not to squash or distort any detail, this is just the preliminary texture. With a small wire loop tool make faint skin texture lines in the clay. Follow the lines in the performer's skin, which are present on the cast and carry them onto the clay. Using a wire loop tool, lightly create directional pores on the surface of the clay over the lines just made. Use a light tapping method and allow the pores to have a random appearance.

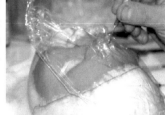

Step 6

Clear plastic can also be draped over the sculpture to create faint lines and subtle textures.

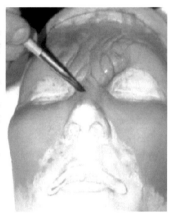

Step 7

As a final step to the sculpture, paint on a layer of plastic film as a sealer. Some artists use a clear spray, but we are using a plastic sealer. Never paint the edge of the prosthetic, as that edge should be as thin as possible.

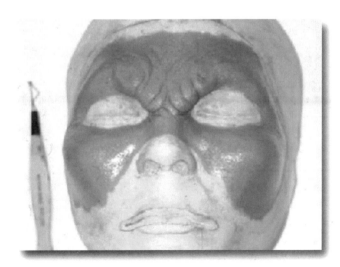

The finished sculpture is now ready to be molded.

The Negative Mold

A negative mold is an impression of a positive form. Creating a prosthetic mold requires an artist to duplicate the sculptural area modeled onto the positive. The prosthetic sculpture is molded in order to produce multiple and exact appliances repeatedly. A facial prosthetic is generally created from a simple two-piece mold, the inner core of the mold called the positive, and the outer impression of the sculpture called the negative. Although prosthetic molds can be more complex due to their shape and size, most traditional facial prosthetics are created using this method, or a variation thereof.

Like the positive, negatives may be created from a variety of mold materials that may be specific to the needs of the artist or appliance material. Ultracal-30 is commonly used to create negatives, and will later be used in conjunction with a mold positive to bake and produce foam latex appliances. It is also common to create negative molds from a dental grade stone, or incorporate the dental stone as a splash coat in an Ultracal-30 negative mold.

Prior to making a negative mold, the exposed surfaces of the life cast positive are to be covered with thin sheets of clay to create what is referred to as flashing. The clay flashing fulfills several technical requirements that become necessary when creating a prosthetic mold. First, the flashing simplifies the shape of the positive mold, making it easier to create a balanced and uniform negative. Second, it creates a negative that is more obtuse, or angled outward and slightly larger than the positive mold. This will prevent problems posed by potential undercuts of the face positive. An undercut occurs when a negative mold wraps around the positive, preventing the positive from being removed. Third, the clay flashing removed when the negative is complete, creates a space or void between the positive and the negative mold. This space allows any excess appliance material to escape from the mold and not be constrained within the area that will create the appliance. Any appliance material, like foam latex, that cannot escape the mold can result in an appliance that has thicker blending edges.

Negative molds, comprised of a cement or dental stone are often created in multiple batches of material referred to as coats. The first layer is called the splash coat. A splash coat is used to duplicate detail, and should be a uniform thickness of one-quarter of an inch. The second is called the reinforcing layer, it is used to strengthen and add support to the mold and its splash coat. Either loose hemp, or burlap cut into strips, can be used for reinforcing the mold. This material is essential to creating a mold that will last a long time. A reinforcing layer is typically no greater than three-quarters of an inch thick.

The final layer is called the beauty coat, used to shape and balance, creating a clean and uniform negative mold. The strength of a negative mold lies in its uniformity. Those comprised of

cement or dental stone are typically no greater that one and one-quarter inches thick. Creating a thicker mold will dramatically increase the weight, which may be difficult to lift and maneuver.

This negative mold will produce an exact copy of the prosthetic sculpture to be duplicated in a foam latex appliance material. It is produced directly over the life cast positive and prosthetic sculpture.

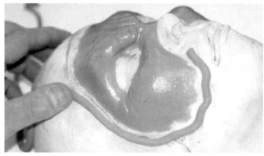

Step 1

Using a clay extruder lay out a triangular clay extrusion. Lay the clay all around the sculpture no greater than one-quarter of an inch. This will leave an exposed area of the positive at the perimeter of the sculpture. This exposed area will create the cutting edge of the negative mold. Be certain that this clay extrusion does not contact the sculpture.

Step 2

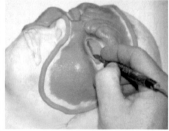

All large areas of exposed cement need to be covered with clay, even the eyelids. Again, do not touch the sculpture with the clay or the extrusion. Lay a pad of clay over the eyelid then cut around the pad creating a clean 90 degree angle from the cement.

Step 3

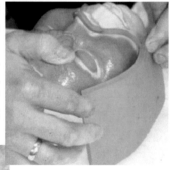

Water based clay can be used over the rest of the cast. Since we are only making a mold of the sculpture area we do not have to worry about the detail on the rest of the cast.

Step 4

The water based clay is laid over the rest of the cast and then angled outward at the bottom. Two square holes are cut into the clay and removed leaving bare cement as touch points for the mold. Notice the exposed cement all around the sculpture; it is important to keep this area free of clay or any debris.

Step 5

Mix up a small amount of Ultracal-30; this will be the splash coat. Place water in the bowl and slowly sift in cement until a dried lakebed effect is achieved. Let it stand for a moment then mix thoroughly.

Step 6

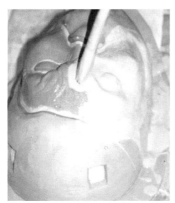

Slowly and carefully brush the splash coat over the entire sculpture, do not trapping any air bubbles against the surface and be careful not to damage the sculpture itself. Once the sculpture is covered work over the rest of the clay area.

Step 7

Work the splash coat over the mold, covering every area. Now build a little thickness by applying more cement over the first layer. Once a thickness of a quarter of an inch is built allow the cement to slightly set. It should be stiff but not hard.

Step 8

Mix up a second batch of Ultracal-30 for the reinforcement layer, using either burlap or hemp as the reinforcement. Dip the burlap into the new mixture of cement and wipe away any excess. Apply the soaked burlap over the entire mold, working out any air bubbles. If using hemp, it will only need one layer, and burlap will need two overlapping layers.

Step 9

Mix up a third batch of Ultracal-30; this will be the beauty coat. This third batch should be just a little thicker than the previous two. Once it is thoroughly mixed, apply to the mold using a rubber kidney tool, a spatula, or a hand. Create a flat top to the mold so it will not rock when laid open. This top layer should be smoothed as it is applied in order to achieve a nice even surface.

Step 10

Let the mold completely cure then turn over. Remove all the exposed clay. A hand planer can be used to round any sharp edges.

Step 11

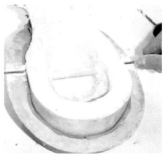

To remove the cast from the negative mold, drill two small holes, one on each side of the cast. Using two screwdrivers simultaneously, gently pry the cast out of the negative mold. Slow, gentle pressure is better than one hard push on the screwdrivers. As soon as the cast moves, slowly pull it free of the negative mold.

Step 12

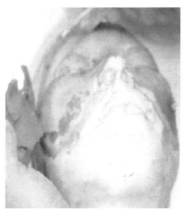

Clean all the clay from each mold. Do not use metal tools since they will scratch the surface of the mold. A wooden tool used very carefully will work well to remove all the clay. Both molds need to be completely clean.

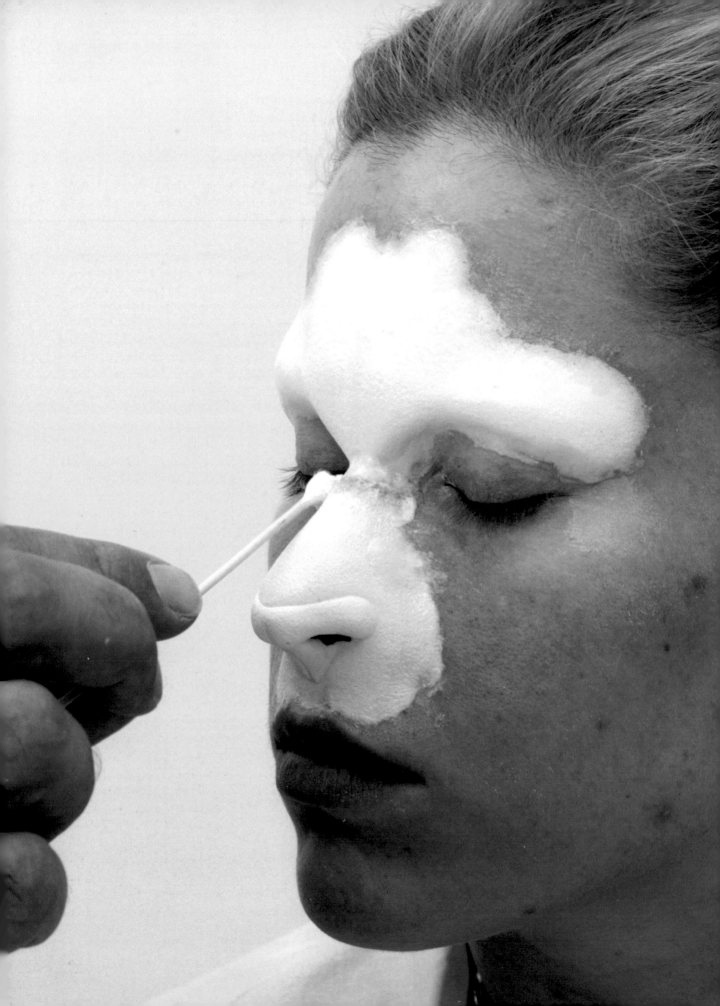

CHAPTER 5

Foam Latex Prosthetics

Foam latex is one of the most common appliance materials used today. These prosthetic appliances are light, dependable, and compress well with the movements of the face and body. Using a simple two-piece mold, a make-up artist can produce numerous prosthetic appliances that might be required for a film or television production. Foam latex is mixed and then injected into the space in the molds left by clay. The foam latex is baked in an oven for several hours and once the mold is opened a prosthetic appliance is removed. This appliance is a custom-made piece designed to fit the person originally cast.

Many companies produce and package foam latex kits for make-up applications. Foam latex kits generally consist of five basic components: foam latex base, foaming agent, curing agent, gelling agent, and mold release.

Foam latex base is essentially a purified blend of natural latex rubbers, suspended in ammoniated liquids. Ammonia keeps the latex liquid while it is packaged, however much of that ammonia is lost as the combined components are blended with a standard kitchen mixer.

Foaming agent is a blend of specially formulated soaps and softeners designed to make bubbles in the foam latex mixture. These bubbles are mixed at various speeds with a kitchen mixer to produce an ultrafine cell structure within the foam latex.

Curing agent is a special blend of sulfur-based additives and conditioners, designed to add durability, bounce, and elastomeric memory. With proper vulcanization, a foam latex appliance will exhibit elastomeric memory when the surface is pressed and released, allowing the foam latex to spring back into the correct shape. Vulcanization is a chemical process in which heat is applied to rubber solids treated with sulfur additives. Vulcanizing rubbers adds strength, and allows the rubber to stretch and bounce back when pulled.

Gelling agent is a chemical additive designed to coagulate the rubber solids in a foam latex mixture at a specific level of Ph. It is introduced into the mixture after the bubbles in the foam latex have been refined and reduced to an ultrafine cell structure.

Mold release is a material that is applied to the interior of a mold.

The manufacturer of the foam latex components provides it with the other chemicals. Mold release allows for the foam latex prosthetic to be easily removed from a warm mold.

Foam latex can be introduced into a mold either by opening a mold and filling it directly, this is referred to as "open-filling" a mold, or by means of "injection". The process of injecting a prosthetic mold requires the make-up artist to drill a hole into the positive so that once closed, the mold may be filled. This hole is called an injection hole. A special tool called an injection gun is used to inject a mold with a foam latex mixture. The gun resembles a large plastic syringe. Secondary holes, although much smaller, may also be drilled into the negative. These holes are designed to allow the air trapped between the positive and negative mold to evacuate quickly. This equalizes the pressure created as foam latex is injected into the space occupied by the trapped air. These holes are called "escape holes". The process of preparing a mold with these holes is referred to as "plumbing a mold".

Prior to preparing the foam latex mixture, the mold should be plumbed, and the positive and negative pieces should be brushed with a mold release. A scale is used to weigh each of the foam latex components, and they are combined in a standard kitchen mixer using a run schedule. A "run schedule", supplied with the manufacturer's foam latex kit, is a suggested formulation and procedural instruction for weighing and mixing a batch of foam latex. The schedule is very specific and precise. Once the foam latex has been mixed and combined, the mixture is used to fill a prosthetic mold. The mold is heated in a special convection oven for several hours to about 185 degrees Fahrenheit. Precise baking time is dependant upon the thickness of the mold and the appliance material. As the foam latex bakes, the mixture produces strong odors, gassing out excess sulfur and ammonia during this time. For this reason, special foam latex convection ovens are used, and are sufficiently ventilated. After the required baking is complete, the prosthetic mold is allowed to cool within the oven until the mold is warm to the touch. The mold is opened carefully, and the prosthetic appliance is removed and ready to apply.

The following is a step-by-step process for making a foam latex appliance. Once the mold is clean it can be plumbed with injection and escape holes, and then filled with foam latex or any other prosthetic material.

Step 1

To get the foam latex into the mold, drill an injection hole in the positive mold. Center the hole in the middle of the area of the prosthetic; it should be located in a thick area of the sculpture. The foam latex will flow into the mold a bit easier if there is room under the injection hole. Drill this small hole all the way through the cast.

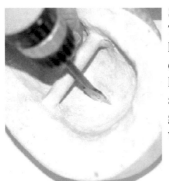

Step 2

Turn the cast over and drill a larger hole using the smaller drill hole as a guide. This hole should be the same size as the nozzle of the injection gun. Only drill this hole half way through the cast.

Step 3

A small piece of PVC pipe can be glued into the hole to make the fit between the injector gun and the mold a little tighter or to elevate the injector hole and make it more accessible.

Preparing The Foam Latex

Follow the manufacturer's directions that come with the foam latex kit; each manufacturer provides different formulas for their particular foam. A gram scale is used to weigh out the various components. The room must be cool, with low humidity. The first is the foam latex base. Pour into a large bowl, following the manufacturer's directions for its size and the type of mixer that will be used. We are using a Sunbeam Mixmaster to mix the foam and the large bowl formula. Foaming agent is the next ingredient to be poured into the bowl followed by curing agent. Gelling agent is poured into a small separate cup and set aside. It will be incorporated into the mixture at a separate time. Place the large bowl into the mixer. Most directions suggest placing the mixer on a low speed for one minute to combine all the chemicals. It is critical to follow a precise schedule. A digital timer is perfect to keep

accurate time. Turn the mixer to a high speed, whipping air into the foam mixture. Once the proper volume is achieved slow the mixer down to refine the foam. This will make the bubbles in the foam latex a uniform size. Slow the mixer down again to ultra refine the foam latex.

Step 4

Slowly add the gelling agent into the mixture over a thirty second period while the mixer remains at its low speed. After the gelling agent is added, use a spatula and turn the bowl in the opposite direction to ensure the gelling agent is thoroughly mixed in.

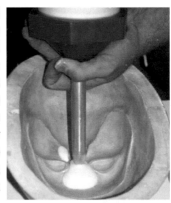

Step 5

Pour the entire mixture into an injection gun. Hold it at a forty-five degree angle as the foam is poured; be careful not to trap air at the end of the gun. The foam latex may be spread or injected into an open faced mold as seen here or use the injection hole, as seen in Step 7.

Step 6

After the open mold is filled with foam, slowly lower the positive mold into the filled negative. The excess foam will squeeze out the sides of the molds. Apply gentle pressure to ensure a snug fit, which translates into thin edges of your appliance later.

Step 7

Here a mold is closed and ready to be injected. The injection gun fits snugly to the injector hole. The trapped air and excess foam will extrude out of the escape holes.

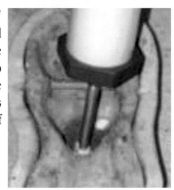

The filled mold goes into the oven to bake. The mold will remain in the oven for an additional hour to cool down properly. The oven circulates heated air around the mold, cooling it slowly. The heat can be turned off at the required time and the oven will still circulate the air around the mold. The injection and extrusion foam can be cut away before opening the mold. Gently pulling on the extruded foam, use a sharp pair of scissors to cut away as much of the foam as possible. Using two screwdrivers, slowly pry the mold open. Gentle pressure is all that is needed to break the seal between the molds. The delicate appliance may rip if the molds are forced open carelessly. Carefully peel the mold halves apart. If necessary, cut more of the extrusion with the scissors, or stick a finger into the mold, gently peeling the appliance from one half or the other.

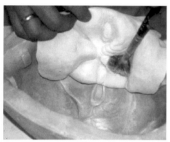

Step 8
Powder the exposed side of the prosthetic appliance. Gently peel up the edge and apply a translucent powder. Since the prosthetic is made of latex there is a chance it may stick to itself. Remove the flashing, the extruded foam, and the prosthetic appliance together.

Application

As a make-up artist, application is the central focus of our craft. The process of creating prosthetics might not appeal to some make-up artists, although valuable information to know and understand. However, it is important to be practiced and current on all aspects of prosthetic application.

In the professional industry, two types of adhesives are used to secure prosthetics to the face or body. The first type of adhesive is a silicone-based adhesive. Silicone adhesives are pressure sensitive adhesives that stick and dry immediately. These adhesives work very well, however they are quite expensive and often thinned with solvents that may irritate a performer's skin. The second type of adhesive is an acrylic emulsion adhesive. These adhesives are pressure sensitive contact adhesives, and easily identifiable by their white color. They are not sticky when wet, and only become tacky when dry. Acrylic emulsion adhesives will turn clear when they are completely dry. Pros-Aide adhesive, manufactured by ADM Tronics, is an example of an acrylic emulsion adhesive.

Under ideal circumstances, when a prosthetic is applied, the blending edges completely disappear into the skin. If the edge of an appliance is too thick, it will not transition well into the skin. Ridge filler may be applied with a palette knife to fill in the edges

that do not disappear into the skin. Many different materials can be used as a ridge filler such as Duo eyelash adhesive, matte gel artist medium, Pros-Aide cream, and other pastes made with Pros-Aide. An inert thixotropic agent, called Cab-O-sil, can be mixed with Pros-Aide adhesive until a thick paste is formed. A thixotropic agent is an additive that is used to thicken a multitude of liquids and gels. It is used in many different industries. Make-up artists have nicknamed this concoction "bondo" or "cabo-patch" for obvious reasons.

PAX paint is a mixture of Pros-Aide adhesive and artist pigment developed to color prosthetics with a flexible, durable paint product that does not smear or smudge. Originally formulated by Dick Smith, the basic mixture of PAX was comprised of equal parts of adhesive and non-toxic artist grade acrylic paints. Today several companies manufacture PAX paint that has been tinted with cosmetic grade pigment, as opposed to acrylic paint. These PAX paints are custom blended to replicate some of the most popular rubber mask grease paint colors.

PAX paints and prosthetic adhesives do require specialty removers. There are many adhesive removers available to the make-up artist and when introducing a performer to a make-up remover, it is advisable to perform a sensitivity test on the skin. Never rely on one type or brand of adhesive remover, as a performer may develop sensitivity after prolonged exposure to a specific remover. Always be prepared with a replacement.

A make-up station is prepared with a prosthetic appliance and all the tools necessary to apply it to the face.

An organized station will create conditions for faster applications.

Step 1
Before the prosthetic is applied to the face, remove the flashing and any injection or extrusion points. The edge also must be carefully checked for an over abundance of thin wispy foam. Do not

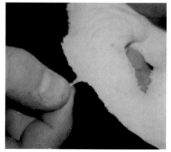

tear off the thin edge, just remove the excess foam that is not necessary to blend the appliance.

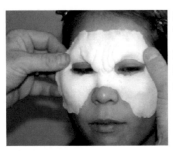

Test fit the prosthetic to the performer's face. Make sure there is plenty of room for the eyes.

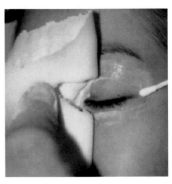

Work back and forth from side to side. This will ensure the prosthetic is going on straight.

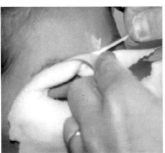

Apply Pros-Aide adhesive to the inside center-most point of the appliance, and then to the skin. Allow to dry thoroughly and press the two dried adhesive points together; this will form the anchoring point for the prosthetic. The Pros-Aide is a contact adhesive that forms a strong bond when applied in this fashion.

The performer should keep their eyes closed when an artist is working around the eye area. As soon as the eye area is attached, powder the eyes, so the performer may open them again, this way they will not accidentally be glued open.

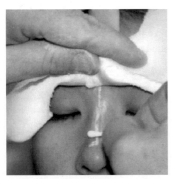

The prosthetic appliance is glued down straight through the center of the appliance. This time do not wait for the adhesive to dry. Simply lift the prosthetic back to the anchor point and apply the adhesive to the skin. Leave the edges undone at this point. The Pros-Aide can be used a variety of ways, either wet or completely dried. The make-up artist can also apply the adhesive to both surfaces to be glued, or to just one surface. Apply the adhesive to both surfaces if there is a problem getting an area to stick. Allow each area to dry completely, and then press them together.

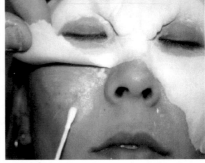

The entire prosthetic must be completely glued down. The only area that might not be glued down is the eyebrow area. The prosthetic only moves and wrinkles properly when it is glued everywhere. The prosthetic then becomes part of the face and moves very realistically.

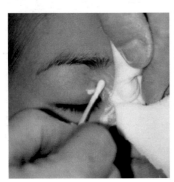

Using the anchor point as a hinge, lift open the prosthetic, then apply the adhesive to the skin. While still wet press the prosthetic into the glue.

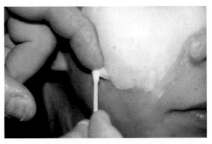

The last area to be glued is the edges. Carefully apply the adhesive under the thin edges, do not fold them over. If by accident an edge has folded over, use a brush dampened with 99% alcohol. The alcohol causes the adhesive to lose its adhesion for a few seconds, allowing for the edge to be straightened. When the alcohol evaporates the edge sticks back to the skin, this time hopefully straight and perfect.

An alternate technique is to lift the edge, apply the adhesive to the skin and allow it to completely dry. Then carefully lay the edge onto the dried glue and press down; the edges are now ready to be blended. If the edges are in good shape, then all that may be needed is to apply a layer of Pros-Aide over the edge to get it to blend properly. A thick edge may require the use of ridge filler. To add texture, apply a layer of Pros-Aide with a textured sponge over the ridge filler. Once the edges are blended, the appliance is ready for color. There are several techniques for applying color to foam latex prosthetics. For this application we chose PAX paint as our base. PAX paint is a mixture of three components. Mix 40% acrylic paint, 40% Pros-Aide, and 20% matte medium. When making PAX paint always mix the color before the Pros-Aide is added. The Pros-Aide is white in its liquid state but it will dry clear.

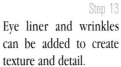
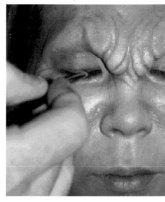

Step 13

Eye liner and wrinkles can be added to create texture and detail.

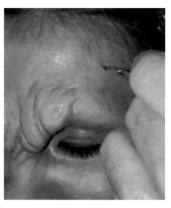

Step 14

Veins and capillaries are added to give the skin a translucent look.

Step 10

Apply the PAX Paint over the prosthetic appliance. The PAX Paint acts like a sealer for the appliance.

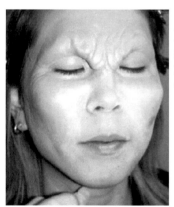

Step 11

Next, use rubber mask grease paint to blend the PAX Paint into the rest of the face.

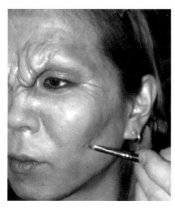

Step 12

Shadows and highlights are applied in rubber mask grease paint over the PAX paint base.

The finished make-up look portrays our performer in a popularized vampire look.

Alternate Foam Latex Prosthetic Application

In this section we describe an alternate technique used to apply and color foam latex prosthetics. As with many make-up techniques there are multiple ways of doing the same type of make-up. The following is a very straight forward way of applying foam latex prosthetics.

First clean the performer's face of any previous make-up or oils. Protect the wardrobe from the materials in the application by covering the performer with a cover cloth. Apply Pros-Aide to skin at the center-most area of the appliance, allowing the Pros-Aide to completely dry. Press the appliance into the dried adhesive on skin; it will hold the prosthetic in position but it will lift easily if the make-up artist decides to reposition the appliance. Lift each side of the prosthetic appliance and apply Pros-Aide under it. Allow the adhesive to dry, and then press the piece into it. Continue in this fashion all the way around the piece, making sure every area of the appliance is glued down.

The edge is the last area to secure. Lift the edge with tweezers and apply the adhesive under it. This time, while the glue is still wet, let the edge fall into it. If the delicate edge accidently folds, use 99% alcohol to loosen the glue and smooth it out. Next, roll a cotton swab over the edge with more Pros-Aide to lay it into the glue then smooth the edge. Once everything is glued down, use a cotton swab to stipple more Pros-Aide over the edge to blend it. Allow the Pros-Aide to completely dry. A hair dryer will greatly speed up this process. Dip a filbert brush

into colorless powder, pressing it all the way around the edge of the appliance. Use a liberal amount of powder. This will help to fill in the subtle step from the appliance to the skin. Remove the excess powder with a brush that is dampened with 99% alcohol.

At this point, it is easy to see any edges that may be obvious to the camera. If there is an edge that is perceivable, ridge filler could be used to cover it. Pros-aide should be applied over the entire prosthetic to seal it and provide texture to the ridge filler. Apply powder to the prosthetic to prevent it from sticking. The application of Pros-Aide over the prosthetic will also help to seal it and will keep the make-up from absorbing irregularly into the piece.

Color the prosthetic appliances using Rubber Mask Grease Paint. The first color should be a shade of red, not a bright one but a subtle red such as one used to add redness to a face. Apply a flesh tone that matches the performer's skin tone. 99% alcohol is used to blend the make-up into the surrounding area. Highlight and shadow the piece and add any accentuations that will be needed. A prosthetic grade make-up, like RMGP, must be used over a prosthetic appliance because of the nature of foam latex. Like latex, foam latex requires a castor oil based make-up that will not discolor or degrade the latex product. The colors that are used in the application will be dictated by the type of prosthetic character that will be created.

MAKE-UP DESIGNORY

STUDENTS

Student
Year

Carly Camasta
2006

tudent
Year

CARPUCINE CHILDS
2006

Student
Year

Emely Webster
2007

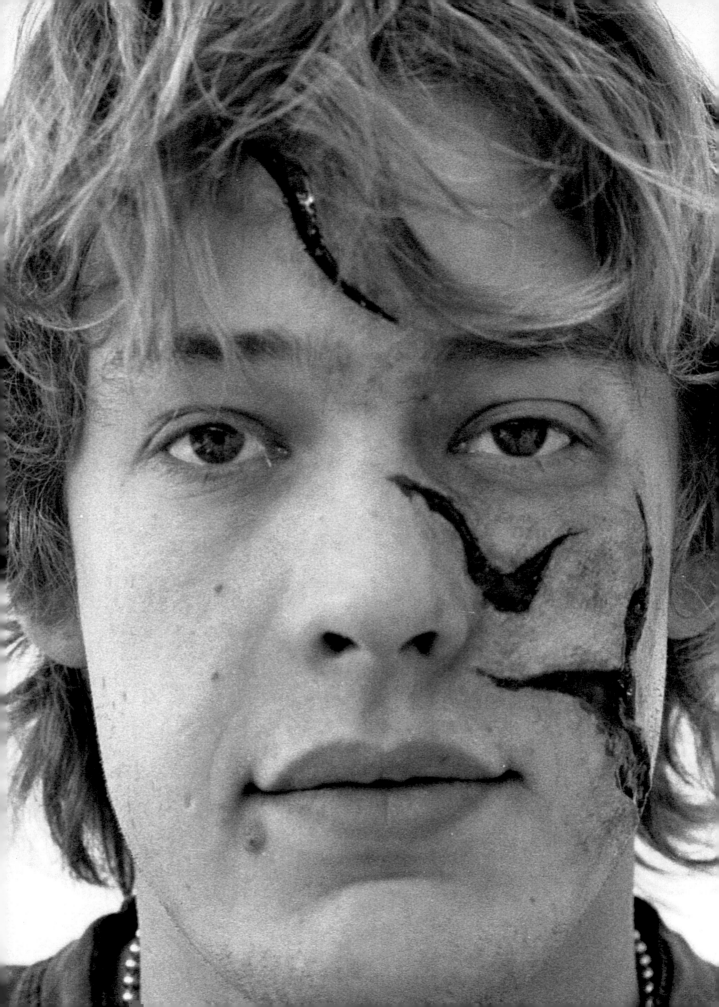

CHAPTER 6

Translucent Prosthetics

Translucent prosthetic appliances are pieces that allow light and skin color to pass through them. Anytime the performers skin color will be incorporated into the make-up, a translucent prosthetic appliance should be considered. The different types of materials that can be used; gelatin, foam gelatin, Pros-Aide transfer and silicone. Silicone will be discussed in a later chapter so we will focus on the first three types. Both gelatin appliances are made and applied in a similar fashion. The Pros-Aide transfer appliances are usually purchased and applied in the same way as a transfer tattoo.

Transfer Appliances

Pros-Aide transfer appliances are translucent, durable appliances that stretch and compress with the movement of the skin. They are colored intrinsically, tinted to resemble a realistic skin tone. These appliances are typically used to simulate injuries or small character traits such as eye bags, nose tips, and earlobes.

Pros-Aide Transfer appliances have had a positive effect on the make-up community, filling a need for appliances that are extremely resilient, quick, and easy to apply. Originally conceived by Christien Tinsley and Keith Vanderlaan working for Greg Cannom's effects company Captive Audience Productions, these appliances were first used on the film "Master and Commander, The Far Side of the World" (2003). This type of appliance also gained notoriety with Tinsley's innovative applications for the film "The Passion of the Christ" (2005). In 2008, the Academy of Motion Picture Arts and Sciences honored Tinsley with a Scientific and Technical achievement award, for his advancement and implementation of transfer appliances into the make-up industry.

Now produced by several make-up effects companies, these appliances have been used in several motion pictures. In "Apocalypto" (2006), the tribal scars, markings, ear and facial piercings were all designed as transfer appliances.

Lunar Effects Studio provided this package of Pros-Aide Transfer Appliances to us. For complete information on their expand ing line of custom or off-the-shelf Pros-Aide Transfer appliances, visit their website at www.LunarEffectsStudio.com.

Pros-Aide Transfer appliances are so fast and simple to apply; even a novice will have an easy time doing it. These appliances are applied similar to temporary tattoos, using water to transfer them to the skin. Their versatility once sealed with a plastic fixative, allows an artist to use a variety of make-up to color the product. Rubber mask grease paints, cream cosmetics and alcohol-based products, applied in translucent washes and stains are most commonly used.

Step 1

Clean the surface of the skin thoroughly. Apply a layer of Pros-Aide adhesive to the surface of the skin and let dry until the adhesive turns clear. This primer layer of Pros-Aide will ensure adhesion in high movement areas.

Step 2

Prepare the transfer appliance by carefully removing the clear plastic film and paper backing.

Step 3

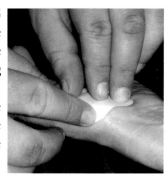

Align the appliance in the desired position, and press the appliance and paper backing onto the surface of the skin. Pros-Aide is a pressure-sensitive contact adhesive; firm pressure will secure the appliance immediately.

Step 4

Saturate the paper thoroughly with clean water. Use a spray bottle, a wet towel or powder puff.

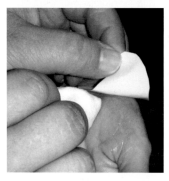

Step 5

After the paper has been saturated thoroughly, gently lift the paper away from the surface of the appliance. Blot the surface of the skin and appliance area to remove excess moisture.

Step 6

Brush the appliance edges with 99% alcohol to blend them into the surface of the skin. Difficult edges may be dissolved using a small amount of cosmetic grade acetone.

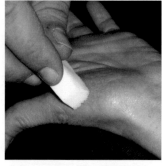

Step 7

Use an orange stipple sponge or a torn white make-up sponge to apply a plastic fixative like Kryolan's Fixer spray. Gently stipple the surface of the appliance and the surrounding area of the skin. Continuing to stipple with the sponge as the fixer spray dissipates will dry the surface to a matte or satin finish.

Step 8

Use make-up that is a bright red and purple color to simulate the trauma and bruising associated with a forceful cut or laceration.

Using a small brush mottle, and texture each color. Use alcohol to thin the make-up product and maintain the translucent appearance of the wound.

Step 9

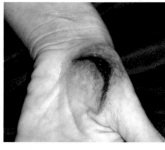

Use a blood red color to simulate the look of a fresh wound. This color tints the wound opening, and textures the exposed tissue of the cut. Black is used to create the illusion of depth along the interior of the wound edge.

Step 10

A small amount of blood will complete the effect. Generally, blood is applied while the character is on-set and in position. This will prevent the performer from smudging the blood, and presents a realistic environment that might establish the direction and amount of blood flow.

Gelatin

There are two types of gelatin being used in the industry today. Foam and regular gelatin are essentially the same except one is foamed so it will behave similar to a foam latex appliance. Gelatin can be used to create just about any make-up effect necessary including prosthetic appliances. Any mold material could be used for gelatin because it does not require backing to cure. Existing foam latex molds could be used, however if there were a need to run foam latex again, it would require the mold releases to be scrubbed from the mold. The following photographic series shows how to make a cylinder mold for a nose appliance. Even though this mold will be used with gelatin it could be filled with any of the various prosthetic materials as well.

Cylinder Mold

A cylinder mold is a small mold that is primarily used for little pieces. It is sturdy and capable of many runs. We have found that gelatin works best in small pieces and the cylinder mold is ideal for clamping.

Life Casting

The life cast procedure is the same as in a previous chapter, however we are casting just the area that is needed. The performer was prepped the same as before with the exception of the bald cap, which is unnecessary since the alginate is kept to the center of the face.

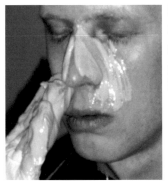

Step 1

Mix up a small amount of alginate and apply it to the performers face. Apply to a larger area than is needed.

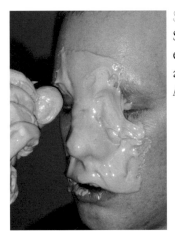

Step 2

Slowly build up the alginate, ensuring all areas are covered and have adequate thickness. Allow the alginate to cure.

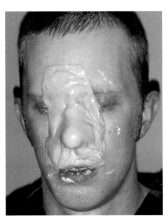

Step 3

Once the alginate has set up, trim the edges with a pallet knife.

Step 4

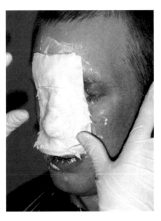

Apply plaster bandages over the alginate. Since the performer is able to breath through their mouth, cover the nostril openings with the bandages.

Step 5

Allow the bandages to cure and then have the performer make facial expressions to break the seal between the alginate and their face. Slowly peel off the cast.

Positive Mold

For a cylinder mold the positive is made in two steps. First the alginate is filled as before with Ultracal-30. It is allowed to cure and then it is floated on top of a base of newly mixed Ultracal-30. This gives the nose positive a thick strong base.

Step 1

The alginate negative is ready to be filled with Ultracal-30.

Step 2

Mix up a small amount of cement and brush in the splash coat. Careful not to trap any air bubbles next to the surface of the alginate.

Step 3

As the cement thickens, slowly build up the thickness of the cast.

Step 4

Build up the cement to create a mound in the middle of the nose cast. Clean away any cement that might be touching the plaster bandages.

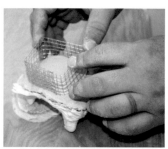

Step 5

Allow the nose cast to cure. Cut a small piece of wire mesh that will be used to reinforce the positive.

Step 6

Bend the wire mesh into a loop and fasten it to itself by bending the wire over.

Step 7

Test fit the wire mesh to the nose positive to make sure that it will fit inside the mesh.

Step 8

Slowly peel off the plaster bandages and the alginate.

Step 9

Clean up the edges of the nose cast with a pair of clippers.

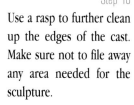

Step 10

Use a rasp to further clean up the edges of the cast. Make sure not to file away any area needed for the sculpture.

Step 11

A metal sculpting tool is used to clean up any air bubbles on the surface of the cast.

Step 12

The materials needed to make the base of the positive. Position the nose cast in the center of a board.

Step 13

Use a piece of rubber molding to form the walls of the mold. Tape the molding to a size half an inch larger than the nose and hot glue it to the board.

Step 14

Mix up a new batch of Ultracal-30 and pour it into the rubber molding. Slip the wire mesh into the cement and continue to pour until it covers the mesh.

Step 15

Wet the bottom of the nose cast and apply cement. Slowly lower the nose cast into the rubber molding and allow it to rest on the wire mesh.

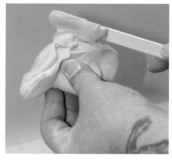

Step 16

Apply more cement around the nose cast until the base is the same height as the edge of the cast.

Sculpture

An oil-based clay is used for the nose sculpture. Since this will ultimately be a gelatin prosthetic we wanted to make a piece that would change the look of the performer and allow their skin color to show through.

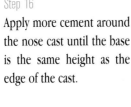

Step 1

Adding small pieces of clay, rough out the nose's general shape.

Step 17

As the cement cures, smooth it out with a damp sponge. Clean away any cement that may have dripped onto the nose cast.

Step 2

Blend the clay together with a finger and fill any low spots with small pieces of clay.

Step 18

Once the Ultracl-30 has cured, pull away the rubber molding.

Step 3

A metal rake is used to refine the shape and to blend the edges.

Step 19

Use a rasp to file any sharp edges off the base of the mold.

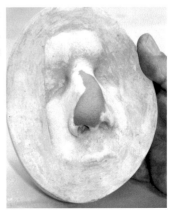

Step 4

Once the shape is finalized, small details such as pores and fine lines are added.

Step 20

The original nose cast is now one piece with the base and is ready to be sculpted on.

Negative Mold

The negative mold is made in almost the same fashion as the base to the positive was made. The positive will need to be prepared prior to making the negative mold. To protect the majority of the surface of the positive we will use a softer oil-based clay to create a space between the two molds. This area is commonly referred to as the flashing. Keys are drilled into the positive mold to create interlocking touch points.

Step 1

Fill a clay extruder with clay. With a triangular tip on the extruder, extrude enough clay to go around the sculpture.

Step 2

The extruded clay makes a retaining wall and is laid around the sculpture. Do not allow the clay wall to touch the sculpture.

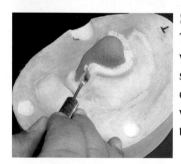

Step 3

The edge of the retaining wall is cleaned up with a sculpting tool. It is angled out to create a strong edge where the two molds will touch.

Step 4

Additionally, the edge is laid around the keys then the area between the retaining walls is filled in with larger pieces of clay.

Step 5

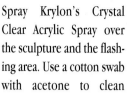
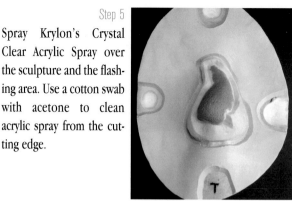

Spray Krylon's Crystal Clear Acrylic Spray over the sculpture and the flashing area. Use a cotton swab with acetone to clean acrylic spray from the cutting edge.

Step 6

The cutting edge is where the two molds will touch. Apply a thin coat of castor oil to the cutting edge to keep them from sticking.

Step 7

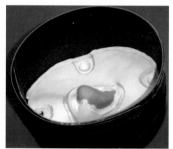

A thin dusting of dulling spray is used as final sealer. Wrap the rubber molding around the mold and tape it around the base.

Step 8

Hot glue the rubber molding to the table and use a small strip of clay to fill the gap from the flashing to the rubber wall.

Step 9

Mix up a small amount of Ultracal-30 and brush it in as the splash coat over the sculpture. Careful not to trap air bubbles against the surface.

Once the entire surface of the positive is coated with the cement, build up a little thickness then pour the mold full.

Step 11

Allow the cement to cure and then remove the rubber molding.

Step 12

Slowly and carefully pry the molds apart using a screwdriver.

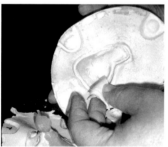

Step 13

Remove all the clay from both mold halves. Alcohol and a soft brush can be used to scrub out any residual clay.

Procedure

In a microwave safe bowl, mix 120 grams of sorbitol with 120 grams of glycerin. Slowly stir in 30 grams of gelatin crystals. In a separate container mix 33 grams of sorbitol with 3 grams of zinc oxide. With an eyedropper, add 9 drops of the zinc oxide/sorbitol mixture into the gelatin. Stir in small amount of Rayon flocking until a desired color is achieved. Stir well and place the bowl into a microwave and cook on high for one minute. Remove and stir. Heat the mixture once more for an additional minute and again remove and stir. Allow the gelatin to cool completely. Reheat the mixture in the microwave slowly and on high one minute at a time. The total amount of time to completely heat up the mixture will vary. The gelatin is now ready to pour. To ensure proper mixing, allow the formula to completely cool and then re-heat it. This will help the gelatin to completely dissolve into the liquids. To minimize air bubbles we recommend placing the melted mixture into a vacuum chamber then de-gassing it prior to pouring. Spray the molds with Epoxy Parafilm as a release agent. Pour the gelatin into the mold and then close. A clamp is used to hold the mold closed and to ensure thin edges in the prosthetic appliance. Open the mold and remove the prosthetic appliance in about 30 minutes.

Step 1

Follow the instructions for making gelatin and combine all the ingredients in a bowl.

Step 2

Heat and mix the mixture until it is smooth and creamy. Let the mixture completely cool after it is mixed. Rayon flocking can be added for color.

Gelatin Formula

This is the standard formula for a gelatin prosthetic material. Several companies sell a pre-mixed formula of gelatin that can be melted and poured into a mold.

Ingredients:
- 30 grams of gelatin
- 153 grams of sorbitol
- 120 grams of glycerin
- 3 grams zinc oxide
- Rayon flocking

Foam Gelatin

Gel-Foam Cubex is gelatin that has been whipped into a stable foam product. Make-up Designory has developed and perfected a formula that is not only stable but also translucent and extremely soft. The Gel-Foam Cubex was developed with the end user in mind for the purpose of creating a viable alternative to foam latex.

Gel-Foam Cubex

The following is a detailed description of how to use the Gel-Foam Cubex. When making new molds, keep in mind there is no need to bake them since gelatin does not require baking as opposed to foam latex. Unbaked molds will last much longer for as a result Cylinder style molds are the best type for gelatin, and we typically use BJB's TC-1630 as our mold material. It has a good detail reproduction and holds up well over time. Large prosthetic appliances can be made, however we found it better to make several small pieces as opposed to one big piece. Both the negative and positive molds should be sprayed with a light coat of Epoxy Parafilm prior to filling with gelatin. Place the desired amount of Gel-Foam Cubex into a microwave safe bowl and heat on high. Heat at one-minute intervals and mix the gelatin in-between heating cycles. This is done so the flocking doesn't become scorched. Repeat this procedure until all lumps are removed. Pour the gelatin into the prepared mold and then close. Use a clamp to hold the mold tightly closed and to ensure thin edges in the prosthetic appliance. In about 30 minutes de-mold the gelatin. Carefully open the mold allowing the gelatin to stick to whichever side it wants to. Usually it will stick inside the negative side of the mold and remain fairly sticky so powder must be used to ensure the edges won't fold over and stick to themselves. Slowly peel the appliance out of the mold as powder is applied. There is usually a small amount of excess gelatin around the edges of the prosthetic appliance, which is called the flashing. Leave only an eighth of this flashing attached to the prosthetic, trimming the remainder away with scissors. The main reason for cutting the flashing is to reduce the weight of the appliance and prevent tearing the delicate edges. Keep the flashing attached until the appliance is glued to the skin.

Making The Appliance

Either gelatin or foamed gelatin can be poured into the mold. The choice will be based on the location of the prosthetic appliance. If it is in an area that will move, it should be made of the foamed gelatin, because it will compress and move better than the regular gelatin. The previous formula would work very nicely for this appliance since it is a nose tip; however we used a cube of foam gelatin

Step 1

The two mold halves are ready to be poured full of gelatin or any other material the prosthetic will be made of.

Step 2

Spray the surface of both halves of the molds with Epoxy Parafilm, a standard mold release that works well to remove gelatin from most surfaces.

Step 3

Slowly pour the melted gelatin mixture into the mold and use a soft brush to work it into the detail. The brush will alleviate any air bubbles trapped on the surface of the mold.

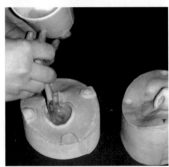

Step 4

Once the mold is full of gelatin quickly close it. Clamp the mold shut immediately after closing, this will ensure the thinnest edges possible.

Step 5

Allow the gelatin to cool and set up for about 30 minutes. Gently pry the two mold halves apart using slow gentle pressure. Forcing the molds apart may tear the appliance.

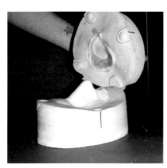

Usually the positive will come out clean. If the gelatin is sticking to both molds try to free the positive first.

Apply Pros-Aide adhesive to the top of the nose and allow it to dry.

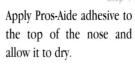

Powder the exposed side of the gelatin appliance before removing it from the mold half. Un-powdered gelatin may stick to itself.

Press the sealed appliance into the adhesive and ensure that it is in position prior to pressing down firmly.

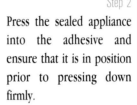
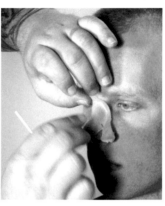

Try to remove the appliance with the flashing. Slowly peel it out of the mold.

Apply adhesive under the edge of the appliance and press it firmly into the glue.

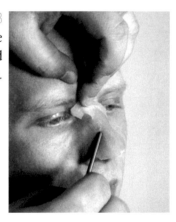

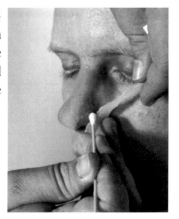

The newly made gelatin appliance is removed and ready to apply, it is resting on the positive mold.

Gelatin Prosthetic Application

Foam gelatin prosthetic appliances have grown in popularity in recent years and will be around for a while. Both gelatin and foam gelatin pieces are applied in exactly the same way. Seal the appliance prior to the application, with two layers of Pros-Aide adhesive and two layers of a plastic sealer. The adhesive and sealer should be applied alternately. The excess gelatin around a prosthetic is called the flashing and should be kept attached until the prosthetic is glued to the skin. To prevent the flashing from accidentally tearing away from the piece, trim away all but an eighth of an inch.

Use a small amount of witch hazel to dissolve the edge between the appliance and the flashing. Allow the flashing to fall away.

Apply more adhesive over the edge to blend it into the skin. Then lightly stipple a thin coat of adhesive over the appliance.

Step 8

A light flesh tone is applied over the nose and concentrated in the highlight areas.

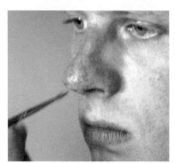

Step 6

Use an orange stipple sponge to apply a plastic sealer over the appliance. Continue to stipple with the sponge to matte the sealer.

Step 9

A darker flesh tone is applied on the sides of the nose as a soft shadow.

Step 7

Using alcohol-based make-up, apply a soft redness to the appliance. The color is applied in a broken pattern.

Step 10

Surface red is added with a brick color that matches the redness in the performer's cheeks.

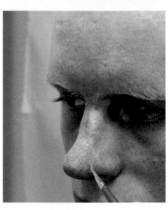

MAKE-UP DESIGNORY

STUDENTS

Student
Year

Anaïs Delgado
2005

Student
Year

Ana Preciado
2005

Student
Year

Amy Solares
2006

CHAPTER 7

Polyurethane Foam Prosthetics

Polyurethane Prosthetic Construction

Prosthetic appliances serve many media including theater and theme park productions. Typically, these types of productions have limited budgets, so making prosthetics that can be re-used is a great way to cut costs. It also reduces the large number of appliances that may be used. There are a wide variety of urethane foams available, however most work in the same fashion as the one illustrated in the photographs. There are two types of foam, rigid and flexible urethane, and which one is chosen will depend on what is required of the foam., There are also a wide variety of densities in those two categories. Rigid urethanes are generally used for hard objects such as horns or some sort of bone effect, whereas, the flexible urethane foam can be used for noses and chins. Realize that the softest urethane foam is not nearly as soft as foam latex and will not move as well either, but it is much more durable and can be re-applied many times.

This is one example of urethane foam, sometimes called cold foam because no baking is required. A wide variety of urethane foams can be found at make-up and special make-up effects suppliers.

Step 1

We are using a plate mold of four noses and the mold is made of TC-1630, a rigid casting urethane. Paint a mold release over both halves of the mold. Refer to the manufacturer directions for an appropriate mold release.

Step 2

Every foam product has its own mixing ratios, so follow the manufacturers' instructions. A triple beam gram scale or an accurate digital gram scale works best to ensure proper proportions. After weighing the required amounts of A and B components, mix the two together.

Step 3

A tongue depressor and a quick hand can be very effective to thoroughly mix the material or use a Jiffy Mixer to do the job without much effort. Do this for 15 to 30 seconds or until completely mixed. Warm the two components for a better foaming reaction. This type of foam must be used in a well-ventilated area and with proper protection, such as a respirator and rubber gloves.

Step 4

Pour the components into the mold as soon as they are thoroughly mixed. The foaming process happens almost immediately, so work quickly.

Step 5

Close the mold by placing the positive onto the negative side, then strap or clamp the mold closed, as the foam will continue to rise and lift the positive mold right off the negative.

Step 6

Allow the foam to completely cure before opening the mold. If the mold is opened too soon the foam may collapse or may stick inside one or both of the halves.

Step 7

To test if the foam is ready to be pulled from the mold, peel up a small section of flashing and squeeze it. If it remains collapsed it needs more time to cure and if it bounces back then it is ready to pull.

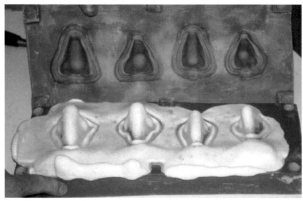

Step 8

Slowly pry the molds apart in the same fashion as a mold filled with foam latex. The finished prosthetic appliance is now ready to be applied.

Application

The polyurethane prosthetic appliance is applied in the same fashion as a foam latex prosthetic appliance. Its durability allows this type of prosthetic to be removed and re-applied several times.

Student
Year
Denise Hernandez
2005

Student
Year
Dani Calandra
2007

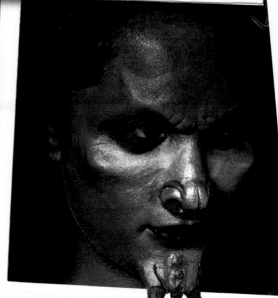

Student
Year
Diana López
2007

CHAPTER 8

Silicone Prosthetics

Multiple Piece Prosthetics

Prosthetic appliances can be made as one piece or as many pieces that overlap. In previous chapters the single piece prosthetic has been used to describe the process of making prosthetic appliances. In this chapter we will illustrate the process of making multiple piece prosthetic appliances. Even though we will be making silicone gel filled appliances, this process can be used for any prosthetic material. Life casting and the positive mold construction start out the same way as all the other types of prosthetics. The sculpture is where things change a bit. Prior to starting the sculpture, coat the positive with two or three applications of Alcote, enabling the sculpture to lift off the positive. Once the positive mold is coated with Alcote and it has dried completely the clay sculpture is started. Cut through the clay with an X-acto knife. The sculpture is kept thin where the cuts are anticipated. This can be done for all of the sections at one time, however this should only be done if the texture is relatively light and there are no details crossing the edge. If there is detail crossing the edge then the sculpture needs to be cut one section at a time. Each section is removed individually and the part of the sculpture that remains is blended back down. A mold of the new area is made. This allows the first section to be applied to the new mold, which has the surrounding sculpture area cast into it. The section is blended into the mold matching up the detail. In this particular series of photographs we cut all the sections at one time and removed them prior to making new molds. Cylinder molds are made of each portion of the face that will receive a sculpture section. The sculptures are transferred to the new molds and blended. Once all the sculptures are in place, negative molds are made-as seen in earlier chapters. The reasons for breaking a prosthetic down into smaller sections are to allow for a more movable make-up, to counteract the shrinkage of materials, and to make the prosthetic a little more comfortable.

Step 1
The sculpture can be done in the exact same fashion as any other prosthetic. This is a finished sculpture for a full-face prosthetic make-up.

Step 2
Using an X-acto knife carefully cut the clay into the desired sections. Cut through the thinnest areas of the sculpture.

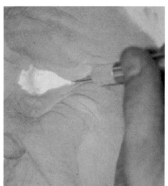

Step 3
Each section is planned from the beginning. The sculpture is kept thin where the cuts are anticipated. Complete all the cuts at one time.

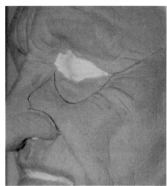

Step 4
Soak the sculpture in a container of water. The Alcote will dissolve in water, which allows the sculpture to be lifted off the positive.

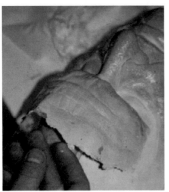

Step 5

Once the sculpture starts to move a little use a thin piece of plastic to help lift the fragile sculpture off the positive.

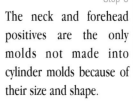

Step 9

The neck and forehead positives are the only molds not made into cylinder molds because of their size and shape.

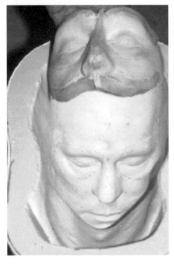

Step 6

All the pieces are lifted off the cast and laid aside. A vacuform copy of the original life cast is generally used to cradle the prosthetics while the new positives are made.

Step 10

All of the sculptures are placed on the positive molds; each sculpture will need to be blended onto the positive and repaired of any damage incurred during the transfer process. Once all the sculptures are repaired, a final texture is pressed into them to unify all the sculptures into one skin texture.

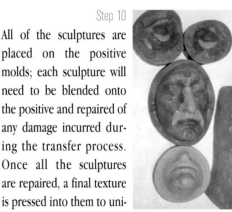

Step 7

A silicone copy is made of the positive mold, and then made of the various areas that will support the prosthetics. In this instance, the mold will be used for the eye bags. The mold is made of a dental stone, but Ultracal-30 or even a urethane molding material could be used.

Step 11

A clay wall is laid around the sculpture and around the keys, leaving only an eighth of an inch of positive mold showing around the sculpture. Also, a rubber dam is wrapped around the positive mold.

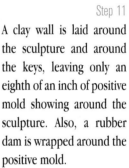

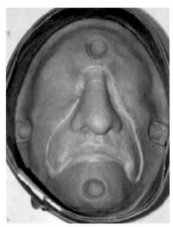

Step 8

The new positive molds are made the same way as in chapter 6 and are now ready to receive the sculptures.

Step 12

The cylinder molds are all filled with a rigid casting urethane. Ultracal-30 or the same dental stone used for the positive molds could be used.

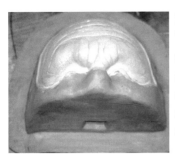

Step 13

The forehead requires the same clay wall around the sculpture; however, instead of wrapping the mold in a rubber dam we created a clay pad around the mold.

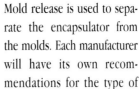

Step 1

Mold release is used to separate the encapsulator from the molds. Each manufacturer will have its own recommendations for the type of separator to use.

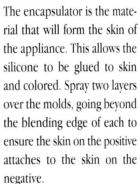

Step 14

The neck is made using the same technique as the forehead. These molds are then brushed up over the sculptures, creating a negative mold that is about 3/4 of an inch thick, following the contours of the sculpture. This is a more traditional molding technique.

Step 2

The encapsulator is the material that will form the skin of the appliance. This allows the silicone to be glued to skin and colored. Spray two layers over the molds, going beyond the blending edge of each to ensure the skin on the positive attaches to the skin on the negative.

Step 3

Carefully close each mold, if the encapsulator sticks and the molds are closed improperly, the skin may stick together in an undesirable area.

These are all of the molds for this multiple piece prosthetic make-up.

Step 4

Tint the silicone gel for all the appliances at one time with color or flocking. Weigh out small amounts of the gel and add catalyst to it, depending on the manufacturer's requirements. Use a large syringe capable of holding enough material to fill one mold and draw the material into it. With the molds tightly strapped, inject the silicone gel into the closed molds until the extrusion holes leak.

Silicone GFA Construction

Silicone gel filled appliances are made with a silicone gel that is encapsulated within a skin-like material. There are several manufacturers of this type of prosthetic material and we suggest doing research to find the best material for a particular job.

Leave the syringe in the injector hole to keep positive pressure inside the mold. After the gel is cured the syringe can be easily removed.

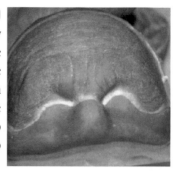

There should not be any large areas of flashing like seen here. Instead the encapsulator sprayed on both the positive and the negative did not stick to itself, allowing the gel to escape.

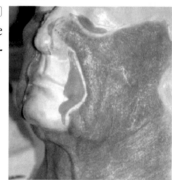

The same is present here but not as badly. This particular piece is still usable.

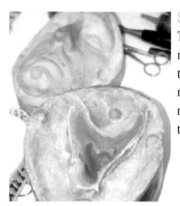

This particular system does not require baking; just let the silicone cure then demold. Slowly open the molds, being careful not to tear the prosthetics.

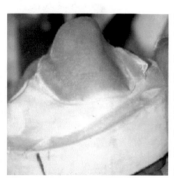

The finished prosthetic is an intrinsically colored appliance. The outer skin moves independently of the inner skin, which is attached to the face and results in very realistic movement.

Silicone GFA Application

A silicone gel filled appliance is applied virtually the same way as a gelatin prosthetic. We did a test with both silicone and foam gelatin, making appliances of each type by running the different materials in the same molds. Once applied, both appliances looked virtually the same. The big difference was that the silicone GFA moved and felt real. This is a step-by-step look at the entire process of how a multiple piece prosthetic make-up should be applied using silicone gel-filled appliances.

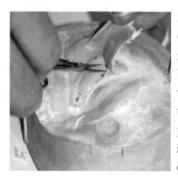

Carefully peel the prosthetic from the positive mold. Usually the piece will stay with the positive because of the extrusion points. These points need to be cut away as the prosthetic is peeled off.

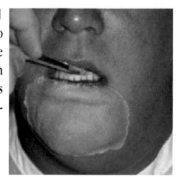

The chin is the first piece to go on, using Pros-Aide adhesive to glue it down and the same techniques we employ for other prosthetics.

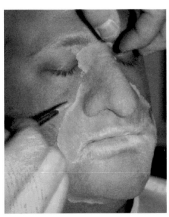

Step 2

The nose and upper lip are next. The entire prosthetic is glued down. Any folded or wrinkled edges straightened with alcohol.

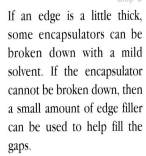
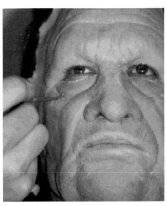

Step 6

If an edge is a little thick, some encapsulators can be broken down with a mild solvent. If the encapsulator cannot be broken down, then a small amount of edge filler can be used to help fill the gaps.

Step 3

The neck and cheek pieces are the trickiest. Begin under the chin first by applying a layer of adhesive to the skin, then to the appliance. Allow both to dry and then press them together. Next, work up each cheek until the whole appliance is attached. Leaving the center-most part of the neck unglued will make it move and look more interesting.

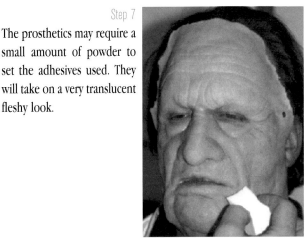

Step 7

The prosthetics may require a small amount of powder to set the adhesives used. They will take on a very translucent fleshy look.

Step 4

The forehead piece is anchored between the brows. Fold the prosthetic forward and apply adhesive to the rest of the forehead, then unfold the piece.

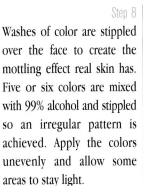
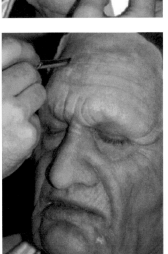

Step 8

Washes of color are stippled over the face to create the mottling effect real skin has. Five or six colors are mixed with 99% alcohol and stippled so an irregular pattern is achieved. Apply the colors unevenly and allow some areas to stay light.

Step 5

The eye bags are applied last. Once all the pieces are attached begin the blending process.

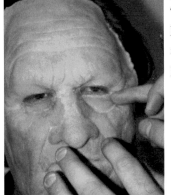
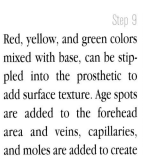

Step 9

Red, yellow, and green colors mixed with base, can be stippled into the prosthetic to add surface texture. Age spots are added to the forehead area and veins, capillaries, and moles are added to create translucency in the make-up.

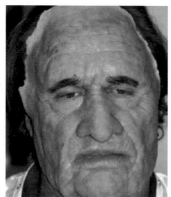

Lace eyebrows are added. The lace is applied with a silicone adhesive, being careful not to mess up the make-up as it is applied. The lips are given a touch of color.

A wig is applied over the actor's head and the top edge of the prosthetic forehead.

The finished silicone gel filled appliance.

MAKE-UP DESIGNORY

STUDENTS

Student   Marissa Walden
Year   2007

Student   Sara Orlandini
Year   2006

Student   Maria Del Rocio Jimenez
Year   2007

CHAPTER 9

Airbrush

Airbrushing Basics

Most airbrushes are designed to allow water-based paints, oils, adhesives, enamels, acrylics, and make-ups to flow through them. Any free-flowing material with liquid consistency can be sprayed through an airbrush.

There are a variety of airbrushes available to make-up artists and we will de-mystify the tool altogether. Many people believe the airbrush is a magic tool, the end-all to any art project. The airbrush is indeed a great tool, but it is just one option amongst the many that are available for an application. Just as we use a sponge or a brush, one is not better than the other it is just different. As make-up artists, we are able to create different effects with the airbrush.

There are many types of airbrushes available from most manufacturers, which usually have three distinct characteristics. The first is either a single-action airbrush or a double-action airbrush. The action refers to the artist's ability to control the air and paint flow. The second characteristic is how the paint is fed into the airbrush, and the last is where the paint and air mix, either inside or outside the airbrush body.

Single Action

The single action airbrush is usually the least expensive available and the simplest to operate. Pressing down on a single trigger causes air and paint to be expelled from the airbrush. There is usually a separate control that allows the artist to preset the amount of paint to mix with the air prior to its use.

Double Action

This type of airbrush is more expensive than a single action and is more complicated in its design. The artist has control over the airflow and the amount of paint with two independent movements of a single trigger. This allows more control of a wider range of effects.

Bottom, Side And Gravity Fed

How the paint is fed into the airflow can vary for both types of airbrushes. The bottom and side feed airbrushes have the paint siphoned from a color cup and into the air stream. They usually have changeable color cups that allow for larger amounts of paint. The gravity fed airbrush has the color cup sitting on top of the tool, which allows gravity to force the paint into the air stream. This type of tool requires less air pressure to get the paint and air to mix.

Internal And External Mix

An internal mix airbrush mixes the paint inside the airbrush, while the external mixes it outside. The internal usually creates a finer mist of paint and the external can spray thicker paint.

Keep the airbrush clean and in good working order and follow the instructions that come with it. An airbrush is a vital tool in any make-up artist's kit. The following are some of the most popular airbrushes on the market. We photographed them assembled and disassembled to illustrate how each must be maintained. Once it is understood how an airbrush is taken apart and put together the easier it is to comprehend its inner workings. This is the best way to become one with the tool. The more comfortable the artist is taking the tool apart, the more at ease they will become with the tool itself. The airbrush rarely needs to be disassembled to this degree; however the areas that may be exposed to paint must be cleaned thoroughly each time the tool is used.

Airbrush Breakdown

There are many airbrush manufacturers and an even wider range of models available. When deciding on airbrushes to purchase research each company and the specific qualities of each airbrush. There is no need for a make-up artist to buy the most expensive one on the market. For the type of work we do most airbrushes will easily fulfill our needs. Ease of assembly and disassembly, use and comfort, price, and what the artist expects will dictate which airbrush to buy. We have included a sampling of the different types of airbrushes used in the make-up industry.

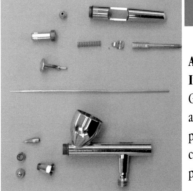

Assembled / Disassembled Iwata Eclipse HP-CS.
Gravity fed internal mix double-action airbrush that is very popular due to its excellent construction and reasonable price.

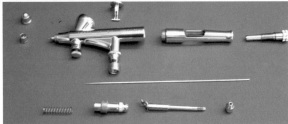

Assembled / Disassembled Iwata HiLine HP-BH

A gravity fed internal mix double-action airbrush that is not only a well-built tool, but it also allows the artist to control the pressure. With a standard compressor this is not as necessary as with the smaller unregulated compressors.

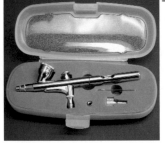

Disassembled / Assembled Temptu SP-35

Gravity fed internal mix double-action airbrush that is an excellent starter airbrush and can be purchased as part of a complete make-up package.

Disassembled / Assembled Paasche H

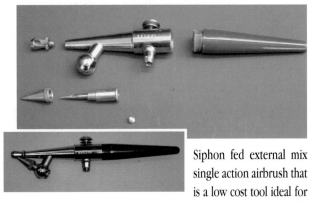

Siphon fed external mix single action airbrush that is a low cost tool ideal for spraying thicker make-ups and adhesives. It also produces a heavier spotted pattern than the internal mix airbrushes.

Assembled / Disassembled Paasche VL

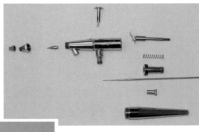

Siphon fed internal mix double-action airbrush. This airbrush has the ability to change the thickness of its needles

and tips to accommodate different types of situations.

Any one of these airbrushes can be used for make-up and are available at most make-up and art supply stores. The price of these brushes range depending on which model and where it is purchased. It is a good idea to have multiple airbrushes in the kit; there should be a variety. With quick connector technology the same hose can connect different types of airbrushes, some of which are offered as a set with additional equipment or make-up.

The Temptu airbrush can be purchased as a package deal that includes make-up and the compressor.

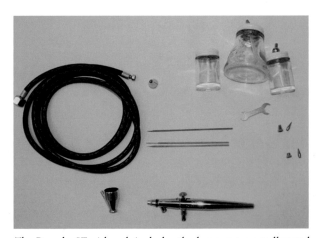

The Paasche VL airbrush includes the hose, extra needles and color bottles.

The Paasche VL is adjustable by replacing certain parts in the airbrush. Most airbrushes come with one setup; however the VL is a little different. Primarily the replaced parts alter the spray pattern of the airbrush.

Changing The Spray Pattern On The Paasche VL

The next four pictures represent the choices in the spray pattern of the tool. The three choices are listed as a numerical value. Number

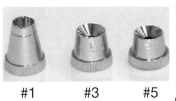

#1   #3   #5

one is the smallest pattern on this airbrush and number five is the largest. When changing the airbrush to a new spray pattern the numbers on all the parts must match.

Here are three air caps close-up; note how they are marked. The number one air cap is marked with a line. Number three and five are marked with their respective numbers, and stamped into the surface.

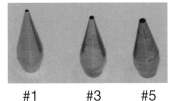

#1   #3   #5

The tips do not have any identifying marks; however there is a visual size difference. The smallest is number one and the largest is number five. Again, these must be used with corresponding needles and air caps.

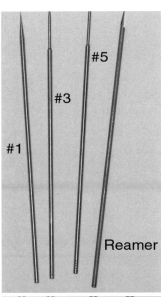

#5
#3
#1
Reamer

The fourth needle is a reamer, used only to clean hardened paint from the inside of the airbrush. Visually, the smallest tip needle is number one and the largest is number five. There are identification marks at the bottoms of each of the needles.

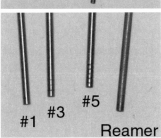

#1   #3   #5
Reamer

This is a close-up of the backside of the needles and their marks. One line going around the needle is the number one, three lines going around is the number three, and five lines going around is the number five.

Air Supply

There are a wide variety of ways to provide air to the airbrush. The most common is a compressor or carbon dioxide gas. The circumstances of the make-up as well as the artist's preference will determine which one is chosen.

Compressors

There are many different types of compressors to choose from. It is important to understand how they work before deciding which one is best. An air compressor does just what its name implies; it uses a diaphragm or a piston to draw air into a chamber and then push the air out at the same rate. For make-up applications, we need to use a compressor that is either silent or very quiet. These types are more expensive than standard compressors and come in a few different forms. One is just a compressor motor, which is turned on and supplies a set pressure. This type can be inexpensive, but does not supply an even airflow. It may be small or large depending on the manufacturer and usually has a limit to the amount of pressure it can provide. The next choice is a compressor with a tank attached. The benefit of this type is an even airflow and a motor that shuts off once the tank is full. It is usually larger in size and may be more difficult to carry around. When choosing a compressor, select a model that allows for control of the air pressure and one that provides a range of pressure for the different types of applications.

Pressure

Adjustable pressure is a valuable asset when choosing a compressor or airbrush. Most make-up is applied at a range of five to ten pounds of pressure, and there are times when we need to lower that to get the airbrush to splatter make-up rather than creating a fine mist. There are also situations when we need to spray a thicker paint or an adhesive through the airbrush which will require higher pressure. So choosing a compressor that will allow for a wide range of effects is ideal. Compressors with the widest range typically cost the most money and we have to balance cost versus pressure.

This is a look at commonly available models of compressors used by make-up artists, starting with the smallest.

The V-One is an example of a small portable compressor that can be used anywhere. It is lightweight and the pressure can be adjusted from one to fifteen pounds. When choosing a portable compressor make sure the pressure is adjustable.

The Silver Jet is a single-person, light-duty compressor perfect for the entry-level artist. Its pressure is adjustable from ten to eighteen pounds. The Silver Jet includes a coiled air hose, Iwata Pistol-Grip Filter, pressure adjustable knob, handle, airbrush holder, pressure gauge and convenient air hose connector.

The Temptu S-One Compressor weighs only 5 pounds; this unit makes a discreet countertop addition to your make-up station and is light enough to carry on location. It features  adjustable air pressure of one to thirty pounds and includes a coiled air hose and airbrush holder.

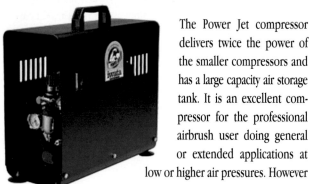

The Smart Jet compressor is perfect for the occasional and professional artist doing general airbrush applications. The compressor shuts itself off automatically when not in use. It is a zero-maintenance, oil-less piston air compressor with a built-in airbrush holder, moisture filter, and a mounted air pressure gauge.

The Power Jet compressor delivers twice the power of the smaller compressors and has a large capacity air storage tank. It is an excellent compressor for the professional airbrush user doing general or extended applications at low or higher air pressures. However it weighs 28 pounds and is typically used in a studio or trailer situation. It is a zero-maintenance, oil-less dual piston air compressor with a moisture-filter, mounted pressure gauge, high-strength braided nylon covered hose, storage tank, tank regulator, and protective outer case.

The Hammerhead Shark compressor features a cooling fan, extra-long heavy-duty electrical cord and highly efficient moisture separator; typically used in the studio. It is designed to handle two brushes

simultaneously, even at different air pressures that can range from zero to one hundred pounds. It weighs fifty five pounds and has a one and a halve gallon tank, moisture filter, a cooling fan, pressure regulator, and wheels.

Carbon Dioxide

Carbon dioxide is a colorless, odorless gas that is made up of two oxygen atoms bonded to a single carbon atom. It can be used as an air supply for situations where there is no electrical power for a compressor or an absolutely silent operation is required. Art stores carry carbon dioxide in spray paint size cans; however they regularly freeze up and run out quickly. The small canisters of carbon dioxide can be kept from freezing by submerging them in about an inch of warm water. Larger carbon dioxide canisters can be purchased from a welding supply company and will last much longer and can be refilled. Canisters come in many sizes; however the ten and twenty pound tanks are the most manageable. A ten-pound tank will typically last about ten hours of moderate spraying and requires a separate regulator to be used. There is a new addition to this category; make-up artists are using small paintball style tanks. Until now a small tank was typically discarded after use and it was impossible to tell how full the tank was. A paintball style tank can be refilled and connected to a regulator that indicates the pressure inside the tank. Cases for Visual Arts in California, sells a pre-assembled system designed with the make-up artist in mind. The two small tanks are pictured below and range from 74 grams to 16 ounces.

The Micro CO_2 has a removable base, regulator with pressure adjustment, a quick connector that fits standard airbrush hoses, and disposable 74-gram tanks. This unit is ideal for on set.

The Mini CO_2 has an over the shoulder pouch, regulator with pressure adjustment, a quick connector that fits standard airbrush hoses, and a reusable 16-ounce tank. It is a compact unit that can be taken anywhere.

Maintenance

All airbrushes and compressors require regular maintenance. Before laying an airbrush aside, even for a short period of time, empty it of all color. Run the proper solvent for the medium being used through the airbrush to clean the residue left behind. There will be times when paint will dry inside the airbrush and begin to affect its performance. To properly clean the airbrush it will have to be dismantled. Refer to the diagrams of each airbrush, usually provided in the instruction booklet that comes with it to ensure proper disassembly and assembly. With the airbrush completely taken apart it is easy to clean every portion of it thoroughly. Compressors with tanks require the tank be emptied of any moisture trapped inside; this will depend on the amount of use. Some compressors require oil to be added to the motor, refer to the manufacturers' documentation for proper use.

Operating The Airbrush

There are three movements that the artist needs to become familiar with when operating the airbrush. Hold the airbrush so the tip of the forefinger rests on the button that activates the airflow. Press down on the button to start air flowing through the brush. Pull back on the button to start the flow of paint. The size of the spray pattern will vary based on the distance from the tip of the airbrush to the work surface. The farther away it is the wider the spray pattern; the closer it is the thinner the pattern.

Airbrush Exercises

Here are some simple exercises we recommend to begin mastering the control of the airbrush. The following lessons are designed for paper and in the fashion described. These lessons should also be carried onto the types of surfaces that will be airbrushed, such as skin, foam, or silicone.

Exercise #1

This exercise is designed to give some basic control over the airbrush. To gain that control, we will use the process of making dots the activity. Start out on paper before moving to skin and use a water-based make-up for easy clean up. Hold the airbrush about one inch from the paper and begin spraying air, and then slowly pull back on the trigger to introduce make-up. Make a small dot with the airbrush and practice this process until dots are placed accurately, without spraying too much make-up onto the paper. Pulling back on the trigger too far will pool the make-up in one spot, creating a puddle. Adjust the size of the dots and their intensity. To accomplish this, allow more make-up to spray out of the airbrush and increase the distance between the airbrush and the surface of the paper.

Exercise #2

This exercise will enable the application of the make-up evenly with the airbrush, as well as blend color from one area to another. When using an airbrush for make-up application, many times we apply base or try to make a body all one color. Again, start out on paper before trying this on skin. White paper will show the areas where more coverage is needed. Practice moving the airbrush left and right over the paper. Make sure to move it this way before releasing any color, otherwise paint will be heavier, creating spots at the beginning and end of the move, leaving a lighter area in the middle. Another technique used to achieve the same result is working in circular motions with the airbrush to create smooth, even coverage over a large area. The final result should be a thin even application of color without any puddles.

Exercise #3

Creating darts with the airbrush is the process of graduating a line from narrow to broad. Practice by moving the airbrush and releasing more color along a straight line and away from the surface. This will create the effect of a fine line that gets wider at one end. The airbrush should always be moving to avoid making a dot at the end of the line. Repeat this exercise until it is comfortable.

Exercise #4

Spray dots in a grid pattern the same fashion as the first exercise. Next, connect the dots with thin straight lines of color that are the same consistency from dot to dot. Continue until any line can be created without over spraying or pooling at the ends of the lines. Again, create another grid of dots and connect them with a curved line. Make sure each line is uniform in thickness.

Exercise #5

The final exercise helps to apply color in layers. Start by spraying a thin application of color in a horizontal line about two inches in height. Next, spray another horizontal line with the same thickness of color about one inch in height, covering the bottom half of the first line. Finally do a third line, again the same thickness of color, but only half an inch in height. The result should be a nice gradation of color from light on top to dark on the bottom.

Continue to practice the exercises described as often as possible. The more these techniques are practiced the faster the airbrush will be mastered. The airbrush can be an extremely versatile tool and a valuable addition to the make-up kit. Feel free to experiment and employ the various techniques we have discussed.

Airbrush Make-up

The airbrush is a tool used to apply make-up; with and not a make-up technique. It can be used to create interesting effects as well as speed up a make-up application. The following is an exercise in highlight and shadow and can be achieved with any other make-up tool as well.

Step 4

Lines are added to the skin for texture by holding the airbrush closer to the skin and moving it quickly across the area. These darker lines should fade at both ends.

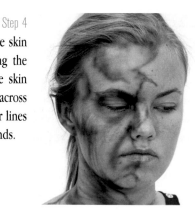

Step 1

Brown make-up is used to do the initial shading and to sketch out the design of the character.

Step 5

Introduce green make-up into the shadows to deepen them and to add color. Move the airbrush closer and then further away as it is sprayed in quick bursts; this will achieve a mottled effect. Green should be sprayed lightly over the face to give it a greenish tint.

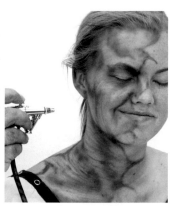

Step 2

Shading is applied under the cheekbone and to the temple area. Continue to apply shadow to all the depressions on one side of the face and neck. Slowly darken the shadows to the depth needed.

Step 6

Yellow make-up is sprayed onto the highlights. Because of the nature of our character, we are applying the color unevenly. Hit all the raised areas first then use the yellow to highlight some of the wrinkles.

Step 3

To create the illusion that part of the face was torn off, add a dark line in a jagged formation to simulate the shadow cast by the edge of skin.

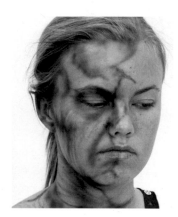

Step 7

Use black make-up to deepen all of the shadows. It is sprayed along the torn off edge as well as in the deepest areas of the facial shadows.

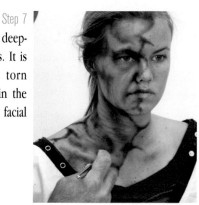

A more traditional tool like a make-up brush is used to add black cream make-up along the very edge of the torn skin. The airbrush creates a soft color and works perfectly to shade an area; however we need the black color to have a sharp edge and more intensity.

Use a larger brush with a deeper red to stipple redness around the eye and to create a little warmth and soreness. The same thing is done at the corner of the mouth and side of the nose.

Different brushes and colors are used to complete small details like dark brown to sharpen the wrinkles and black to line the eye. Use teal for veins and red for small capillaries.

The look is carried into the performer's hair, using the airbrush to spray a little white and a small amount of black. This creates the effect of dull, unhealthy hair.

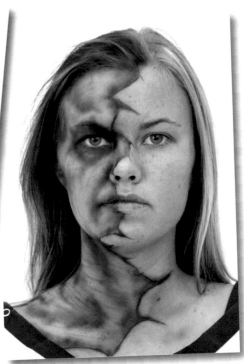

Airbrush Prosthetics

The prosthetic portion of this make-up is done exactly as it was explained in previous chapters; the difference is in how we apply the make-up. It is possible to use the airbrush to do the bulk of the make-up or to use it to create the subtle nuances. Prosthetics may limit the types of make-up used. There is a plethora of options, but in the end it is what works best for the artist should be chosen.

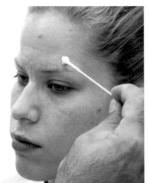

Step 1

Prior to using any glue it is important to see how the prosthetic appliance fits around the eyes and over the eyebrows. Once the position is established remove the prosthetic and apply the adhesive.

Step 2

Apply the adhesive to the skin and to the inside of the prosthetic appliance. The adhesive can be used on the skin or the appliance only, however, for the best bond we recommend using it on both surfaces.

Step 3

Press the prosthetic appliance onto the skin, the adhesive acts as contact adhesive and will bond instantly upon contact. Press firmly as the prosthetic is positioned.

Step 4

Lift the edge of the prosthetic appliance and apply adhesive behind it and carefully lay the delicate edge into the adhesive.

Step 5

With a brush and a small amount of alcohol work the edge until it's straight and smooth. The alcohol will allow the edge to lift and straighten without damaging it.

Step 6

Use a small amount of Pros-Aide with a cotton swab and apply the adhesive over the edge of the prosthetic appliance. Lightly stipple the adhesive on with the cotton swab to blend the edges into the skin. Slowly building up the layers until it is perfectly blended.

Step 7

Powder the edges thoroughly before moving on. Using a brush, press the powder onto the edge and make sure every exposed bit of adhesive is well covered.

Step 8

The nose is applied in the same fashion as the forehead. One thing to keep in mind is to test fit both prosthetic appliances at the same time so it will be known which one to apply first. Spread the adhesive over the center area of the nose and the inside of the prosthetic appliance.

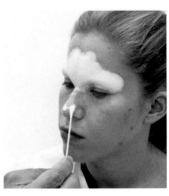

Step 9
Once the adhesive is dry, press the prosthetic appliance to the nose and ensure that the nostrils are lined up properly.

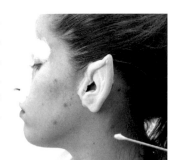

Step 14
Apply adhesive behind the edges of the prosthetic appliance and press them down. Again, you can blend the prosthetic appliance by using more adhesive to soften the edge.

Step 10
Lift up on the edge of the prosthetic appliance and apply adhesive on the skin. Then press the edge into the adhesive.

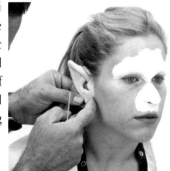

Step 15
Repeat this procedure for the other ear. Once all the prosthetic appliances are adhered and well blended, apply a layer of adhesive to seal them. This will keep the make-up from soaking in irregularly.

Step 11
Apply adhesive over the edges to blend them down, with a brush press powder into the edges.

Step 16
Powder the appliances thoroughly before proceeding. Use a powder puff to ensure that the adhesive has been powdered completely.

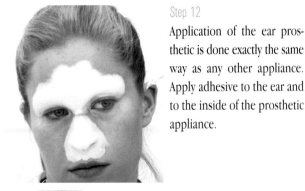

Step 12
Application of the ear prosthetic is done exactly the same way as any other appliance. Apply adhesive to the ear and to the inside of the prosthetic appliance.

Step 17
Notice how much yellow the facial appliances have than the ears. The ear prosthetic appliances have been tinted a color in the mixing process of the foam latex, whereas, the facial appliances are the natural foam color. To counteract the light yellow color of the appliances use a brick colored rubber mask grease paint.

Step 13
Press the prosthetic over the actual ear and be extra careful not to trap hair under the appliance. 99% alcohol can be used to pull out any stray hairs or to straighten out any problem edge.

Step 18
Apply the brick color only on the prosthetic appliances. Powder the rubber mask grease paint completely before adding another color, otherwise the red will mix with the base color and turn it to a funny shade of pink.

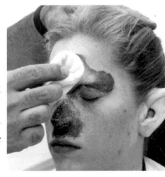

Base color is now applied to the prosthetics by mixing a few shades of the rubber mask grease paint together and then stippling them over the red, and carefully blending into the surrounding skin.

Step 20

The ears, because they are already tinted a skin tone, do not need the initial red color added. However, we still apply the same base color over them.

Step 21

Apply powder over the rubber mask grease paint make-up to create a good base for the airbrush make-up. As another option, we could apply Pax Paint to the prosthetics and then airbrush more Pax Paint on top of that.

Step 22

We are using a Paasche VL airbrush to apply the make-up, but any double-action airbrush will work. Test the airflow of the airbrush on the performer prior to spraying any make-up; this will help the performer to become accustomed to the sensation of the air blast. The compressor is set at about six pounds of pressure.

Step 23

White make-up is lightly sprayed down the center of the face. When working near the eyelids angle the airbrush down so make-up is not forced under the lids. Also, when spraying around the nose and mouth ask the performer to take a breath and hold it until that area is sprayed.

Step 24

Work the white across most of the highlight areas and through the center of the face and neck, spraying small amounts at a time to ensure an even application.

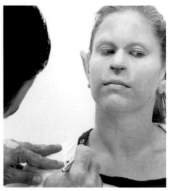

Step 25

Use water to clear the airbrush of any excess white. Mix up a deep reddish purple color to spray along the hairline lightly to create a soft effect.

Step 26

Use the same color to create a more intense look by moving a little closer with the airbrush and allowing more paint to flow. Simply pull back a little further on the trigger to achieve this.

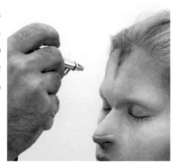

Step 27

Use the same color to shadow the sides of the nose and to deepen the eyes. What is nice about the airbrush is the ease of laying the colors on, and the way they overlap.

Step 28

To create texture, add a dark purple color in a tight spotted pattern over the red. Stencils could be used at this point to create interesting textures.

Step 29

The purple color is also used to deepen some of the shadows inside the ear and along the neck area.

Step 30

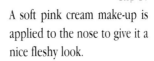

A vibrant red is sprayed over the top of the performer's hair. Streak the color into the hair to mix with the natural color. Spray black into the base of the hair for depth at the roots.

Step 31

A soft pink cream make-up is applied to the nose to give it a nice fleshy look.

Step 32

A deep purple eye shadow is applied over the lids to define them and create drama.

Step 33

The same soft pink color, but this time a lip make-up, is applied to the lips to finish off the make-up.

CHAPTER 10

Bald Cap

Introduction To Bald Caps

A bald cap is used for a variety of reasons, the obvious one to make a performer look bald, but it can also be used under prosthetic appliances as a base. When used under an appliance the cap is usually made of latex and generally does not have to be applied perfectly. When the cap is applied for the purpose of making someone look bald, every step must be taken to apply it as flawlessly as possible. The first step in using a bald cap is to decide which type of cap will be used and the medium it will be seen in (i.e. film, television, or stage). There are three types of bald caps that can be utilized in order to create the effect of a baldhead; vulcanized rubber, a vinyl plastic or foam latex.

The rubber and vinyl have an inherent problem; the back of the head is missing the occipital bone. On a real baldhead there are lots of dents and bumps, and at the base of the skull there is a bony protrusion called the occipital bone. A bald cap is glued on only at the edges because the hair is in the way. So wherever there is hair the cap is very smooth, which really limits the production's ability to shoot the back of the head. If the cap is for a variety show like "Saturday Night Live" or "Mad TV", in which the cap is used for a small segment, then it doesn't matter if the occipital bone is present. However if the cap is for a film and the person needs to look believably bald, then there are a couple of ways it can be done. Apply a rubber or vinyl cap and then a prosthetic to the back of the head to simulate the occipital bone, or use a foam latex cap that is specially made for the performer, with all the details added since it is a sculpted prosthetic. Often times a production will ask the performer to shave his or her head, particularly if the bald person has a major role in the film. If it is a small part, a bald cap will be used, but it is very important to explain to production the limits and the advantages of each type of cap. This will enable production to make an informed decision about which cap to use and being very careful of the way the cap is shot. Proper communication will ensure everyone involved will know what to expect from the bald cap.

Rubber Bald Caps

A rubber cap can be made from almost any vulcanized latex available. We have found Pliatex Mold Rubber, which is used as a molding compound, to be the strongest while staying extremely thin. Pliatex Mold Rubber is available at most art stores. This type of cap may be purchased pre-made or can be made fairly easily using a bald cap form. Most make-up suppliers either carry a rubber bald cap bearing their name or one made by an outside source. Another latex cap, available at most costume and Halloween-type stores, is the Woochie Bald Cap. The other choice is to make a cap from Pliatex Mold Rubber, using a bald cap form. Make-up Designory and Kryolan both offer a reasonably priced form. Because this cap is made of rubber it is important to remember only rubber mask grease paint can be used to color it.

Vinyl Bald Caps

A vinyl cap, sometimes referred to as a plastic cap, is made of a vinyl acetate mixture dissolved in MEK and acetone. Made flexible by the addition of a chemical plasticizer, vinyl caps are not as flexible as rubber caps. Rubber has very good memory, which means it can be stretched and it will return to its original shape. Vinyl on the other hand will stay stretched out. A vinyl cap can be purchased from any of the make-up suppliers. The edges are very thin and can be melted down with acetone to achieve an even thinner application. As this cap is not rubber, regular make-up can be applied to it.

Foam Latex Bald Caps

A foam latex cap is just what it sounds like, latex that is foamed. It has been the industry standard for many years when referring to a prosthetic appliance. However there has been a higher demand for very realistic make-ups and foam latex is now being used to create a realistic bald look. It is very different from the other bald caps, which come in generic sizes. The foam latex cap has to be custom made for each performer and follows the same principles of any other prosthetic appliance. As a matter of fact, a rubber bald cap is applied first and then the more realistic foam latex is applied over it. Coloring a foam latex cap is the same as coloring a rubber cap or a prosthetic appliance; both are made of latex. Pax paint is another product that can be used to paint latex products; although it cannot be purchased it has to be made. The ingredients are 40% Pros-Aide adhesive, 40% acrylic paint, and 20% matte medium. The nice thing about Pax paint is the cap can be pre-painted long before it is applied to the performer. Because it's made with Pros-Aide, it is important to powder the paint thoroughly after it is dry.

Rubber Cap Construction

The following is a step-by-step procedure for making a rubber bald cap using Pliatex Mold Rubber and a MUD Bald Cap Form. Prepare a white sponge for the application by ripping the end off, so a rough surface is left. This will leave an uneven texture on the surface of the cap.

MUD bald cap form

Step 1

Using Pliatex Mold Rubber, apply one layer of rubber to the form. Start at the crown of the bald cap form and work down towards the face and the neck.

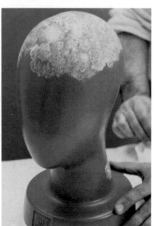

Step 2

Be very careful not to allow the sponge to dry out. If the sponge dries out it will stick to the latex on the bald cap form.

Step 3

Apply thin and even layers, which will dry much faster than thick ones.

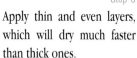

Step 4

Map out the application, making sure latex is applied everywhere.

Step 5

As the latex dries it will begin to turn clear.

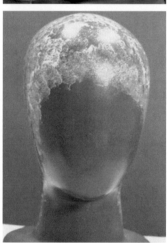

Step 6

Allow the latex to dry thoroughly before continuing. Use a hair dryer to speed up the drying time.

Step 7

Start each layer at the top and work down. Do not rub the latex on or it will tear the first layer. Apply the latex with a stippling motion, carefully moving the latex around the bald cap form.

Step 8

A total of six layers should be applied to the form. Each layer should be applied "inside" the edge of the last layer applied. Keep the edges thin where the blending edge will be.

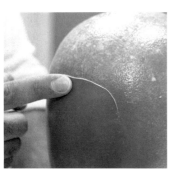

Step 9

We recommend six layers of Pliatex Mold Rubber over the bald cap form. How thick or thin the layers are made will dictate how many are needed.

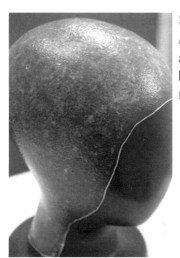

Step 10

Once all six layers are complete and the latex is completely dry, use a finger to roll the edge onto itself. Work all the way around the cap.

Step 11

After the cap is completed and removed, the artist will be able to assess if more or fewer layers are necessary.

Step 12

Powder the entire cap with a powder puff, being very careful to not wrinkle or damage the surface.

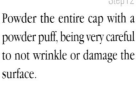

Step 13

Grab the edge by the rolled end and slowly peel the cap back as powder is applied beneath. Slowly move around the edge of the cap until two inches of the edge is pulled back and powdered.

Step 14

Continue around the cap until it is completely removed from the edge of the bald cap form. This helps prevent the edges from sticking to each other.

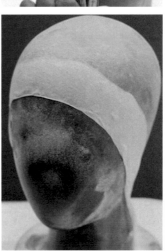

Step 15

Push the brush under the cap along the sides, leaving a strip down the middle of the bald cap form.

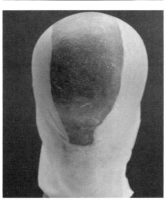

Step 16

Slowly peel off this strip and powder. By undoing the sides first, the center strip comes off easily.

Step 17

Turn the cap inside out and place it back onto the form. Powder the inside of the cap liberally with a powder puff, this will ensure the cap is thoroughly powdered. This is a good time to gently pull apart and re-powder any area of the cap that might have stuck together

The newly created cap is now ready to use. It is recommended that this cap is used prior to making another cap. A great deal is learned after applying the cap that was just made.

Rubber Bald Cap Application

Latex

The most important thing to remember before starting is that this application will be fun. Sit the performer in a chair that elevates them to a comfortable height for the artist. This application will take about ninety minutes, so standing upright is very important. Have the performer sit in an upright position as far back in the chair as possible, and wear a shirt that allows plenty of access to the neck area. Combing the hair first will keep it from tangling. Wet the hair using a spray bottle filled with water and comb it back to lie down

as flat as possible. Taking control of the hair is the first challenge of a bald cap and since this is a rubber cap, most hair gels and hair products in general, will adversely affect the cap and its application. We found plain water to be most effective when utilizing a rubber cap. Do not make the hair overly wet, the excess water can cause problems later on. Clean the inside of the bald cap of any residue powder or debris by wiping it out with 99% alcohol on a tissue. Short hair is the easiest to work with when doing a bald cap and a performer with short hair is usually chosen. The hair is sprayed with water and slicked back. For a performer with long hair we have a few choices. First, the hair can be wrapped around the top of the head to contain it inside the bald cap. The biggest problem with this method is the hair will add bulk to the head and may make the performer look like an alien. Another option that we like, is using a ponytail to hide the hair. Wet the hair and slick it back to put it in a very high ponytail. The ponytail is usually located just below the occipital bone. The high ponytail will help control the hair behind the ear. The hair is then wrapped in a plastic wrap to protect it from the adhesive, and along with the ponytail will be smashed flat once the bald cap is applied.

Preparing short hair

Preparing long hair

Fitting The Cap

Contrary to popular belief, size does matter! If given a choice, it's better to pick a bald cap that is somewhat small, rather than one that is too big. It is essential to position the cap to fit the crown of the head and lie flat against the nape of the neck. This will alleviate wrinkles at the sides and back of the bald cap. A cap that is too large will require a little cutting and some patching to ensure a proper fit. A cap that is rotated too far forward will make the back of the cap flare away from the neck and if it is rotated too far back it will have horizontal wrinkles along the nape of the neck. Clean the skin with 99% alcohol to ensure the cap will stick to the skin.

Step 1

Slipping the cap on the head: stretch the bald cap to ensure proper placement on the crown of the head.

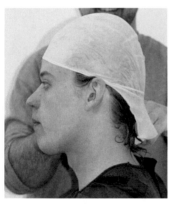

Step 2

Position the cap so there are no wrinkles at the neck area.

Attaching The Cap

Choosing the right adhesive is just as important as choosing the right size cap. Of all the choices available, Pros-Aide seems to work the best. Pros-Aide is a contact adhesive that is most effective when applied to both surfaces, allowed to dry and then pressed together. The front anchoring point is the first place to apply adhesive.

Step 1

Lift the front edge and apply Pros-Aide to the skin and to the cap. Apply it to the center of the forehead and to the inside of the cap and allow it to dry. Press the two surfaces together, this anchor point will be placed under a lot of pressure, so having a strong bond is essential.

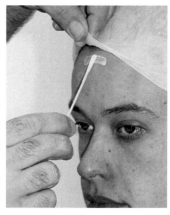

Step 2

Apply Pros-Aide to the back of the bald cap for the back anchor point. Tip the performer's head back slightly and apply Pros-Aide to the back of the neck. Allow both sides to dry completely and then press together.

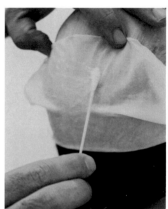

Step 3

Attach the back of the cap to the back of the neck. Tip the head back as the cap is pulled down to ensure a tight fit. When the performer straightens their head the cap will be placed under tension and will be wrinkle free.

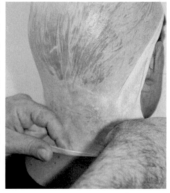

Step 4

Using a make-up pencil make a mark above the ear where it attaches to the head and run the mark down behind the ear. Remember to stretch the bald cap down over the ear and into position as the line is drawn.

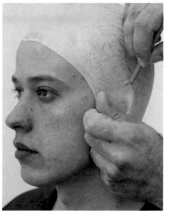

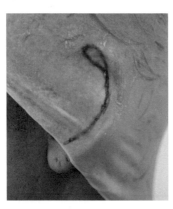

This is the finished mark with the bald cap in a relaxed position.

Cut along the marked line being careful not to create little jagged edges, as these may become large tears.

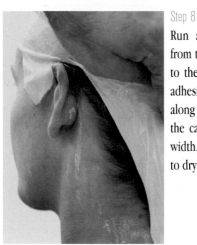

Run the scissors along the line as opposed to making cuts. The material is very soft and will tear easily.

Run a band of adhesive from the back anchor point to the top of the ear. The adhesive should be applied along the hairline and to the cap, about 1/2 inch in width. Allow the adhesive to dry.

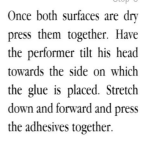
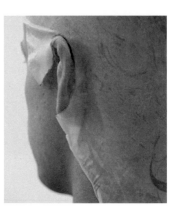

Once both surfaces are dry press them together. Have the performer tilt his head towards the side on which the glue is placed. Stretch down and forward and press the adhesives together.

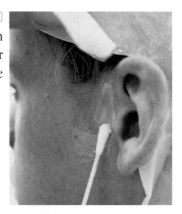

Apply adhesive to the skin from the top of the ear around the sideburn to the front anchoring point.

We usually make the adhesive spot bigger on the bald cap, providing a little more room to stretch and reposition if necessary. The dried adhesive will not bond to the hair.

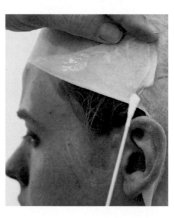

Pull down and forward to alleviate any wrinkles around the ear, pressing the two dried surfaces together. This is what the finished side of the bald cap should look like. Repeat the steps for attaching the bald cap on the other side

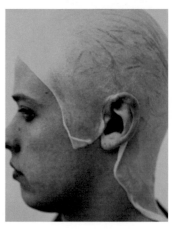

Trimming the Cap

Trim the edge of the cap with a pair of scissors by pulling the cap up and out of the adhesive.

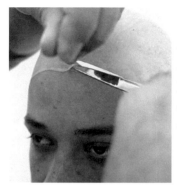

Step 1

Lift up on the edge to pull the cap out of the adhesive. Cut away the excess and lay the newly trimmed edge back down into the adhesive.

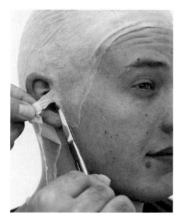

Step 2

Trim the edge all the way around the cap and make sure it is jagged and uneven, this will help to blend it.

Blending The Cap

There are not many chemicals that easily dissolve rubber. Some make-up artists are using naphtha to melt the edge of the rubber cap. Naphtha is a volatile chemical solvent, which works, but it is a little rough on the skin. Another way to get the edge to blend is to apply something that will build the skin up to the same level as the surface of the cap. There are many ridge fillers available and the choice of product is usually the preference of the artist. It is very important to keep the ridge filler off the cap, because if it is applied to both the skin and the cap it will not actually fix anything, only make the edge bigger. Ridge filler is used to fill in the edge created by the cap as it sits on top of the skin. Use a pallet knife to apply it on the skin and sweep it up to the edge of the cap without going over. Apply all the way around the cap. To match the texture of the cap to the skin, tear a white sponge and stipple latex across the edge. Two or three layers may be needed to completely cover the edge. Once the latex is dry powder it.

Step 1

Apply ridge filler to the edge of the bald cap. Slowly build it up to the desired thickness.

Step 2

Use a torn white sponge to stipple latex over the edge of the cap. The texture will match that of the cap.

Coloring The Cap

This critical step can make a bad application look good. Mix a perfect base match using rubber mask grease paint. It is very important to mix the right base color, as it is the base for the entire make-up. Use a pallet knife to spread the base color onto the cap. Do not use too much; a little will go a long way. Mix the colors together on the head and blend into the surrounding skin. Paint shadow under the jawbone, beneath the cheekbone, into the temples and onto the forehead. Wherever possible, apply the shadow across the edge of the cap, which will help to further blend the edge. The highlight should be placed on top of the cheekbones and along the bone structure that makes up the eye sockets. Powder the highlights and shadows at one time. With an orange stipple sponge, stipple at least three different shades of base color onto the cap: a lighter, a darker, and a base match, giving the cap its needed texture. This will also help to soften the highlights and shadows and aid in blending the edge. Once more, using the orange stipple sponge, apply small amounts of both blue and green mixed with the base color. This will give the bald cap that translucent skin quality. A small amount of mustard yellow may be needed to help the colors blend. Finally, apply a brick color to the cap to give it the necessary redness of skin; do not be afraid to use a lot. Both film and television will remove some of the red so it is desirable to use a little more than what seems to be right. Lightly powder the cap, when finished, with a translucent powder.

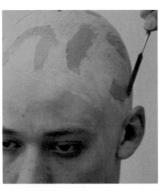

Apply a couple of different shades of base to the cap. Choose colors that match the performer's face.

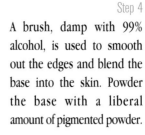
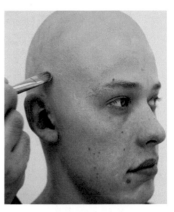

Step 4

A brush, damp with 99% alcohol, is used to smooth out the edges and blend the base into the skin. Powder the base with a liberal amount of pigmented powder.

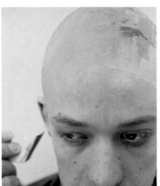

Step 2

With a white sponge or a brush, mix the colors on the head. Stipple the colors together, blending and moving over the head.

Step 5

Apply a shadow and highlight color to the cap with a brush. It is okay to go a little darker than normal, because the highlights and shadows will be covered with more base colors.

Step 3

The colors applied begin to look spotted and textured, just like real skin.

Step 6

Three base colors are stippled into the cap to give realistic texture.

Vinyl Bald Cap Application

The vinyl bald cap application is almost identical to the rubber bald cap application with a few exceptions. We have re-written the entire procedure to illustrate the differences.

Preparing The Performer

Sit the performer in a chair in an upright position that elevates them to a comfortable height for the artist. The performer should be wearing a shirt that allows plenty of access to the neck area. Wet the hair using a spray bottle filled with water, and comb it back to lie down as flat as possible. Gafquat is an excellent choice to flatten and control the hair so it will not interfere with the cap application; it can be thinned with water and applied over well-combed, wet hair. Additionally, Gafquat can be applied full strength along the hairline with a comb or toothbrush. Clean the inside of the bald cap of any residue powder or debris by wiping it out with 99% alcohol on a tissue and slip cap on the head.

Fitting The Cap

The same applies to a vinyl bald cap as it does to a rubber bald cap. If you are given a choice, it's better to pick a bald cap that is somewhat smaller than one that is too big. It is essential to position the cap to fit the crown of the head and to lie flat against the nape of the neck. This will alleviate wrinkles at the sides and back of the bald cap. A cap that is too large will require a little cutting and some patching to ensure a proper fit. A cap that is rotated too far forward will make the back of the cap flare away from the neck and if it is rotated too far back it will have horizontal wrinkles along the nape of the neck. Clean the skin with 99% alcohol to ensure that the cap will stick to the skin.

Attaching The Cap

The front anchoring point is the first place to apply adhesive. Apply Pros-Aide to the center of the forehead and the inside of the cap and allow to dry, and then press together. For the back anchoring point, tip the performer's head back slightly and apply the adhesive to the back of the neck and again to the inside of the cap. Allow both sides to dry before pressing together. Tipping the head back as the cap is attached will ensure a tight fit. When the performer straightens their head the cap will be placed under tension and will be wrinkle free.

Mark one ear with a make-up pencil as the bald cap is stretched down over the ear. Mark right above the ear where it attaches to the head. Run the mark down behind the ear and cut along the marked line. Be careful not to create little jagged edges as they may become large tears. Glue the ear down by applying Pros-Aide

to the skin from the back anchoring point up to the back of the ear. The adhesive should be applied along the hairline, about 1/2 inch in width. Apply Pros-Aide to the cap from the back anchoring point to the back of the ear and have the performer tilt their head towards the side the glue is placed. Stretch down and forward and press the adhesives together. The front of the ear is the next area to be glued. Apply adhesive to the skin from the top of the ear, around the sideburn to the front anchoring point and to the inside of the cap. Allow both sides to dry, pull down and forward to alleviate any wrinkles around the ear and press the two surfaces together. Repeat the steps for attaching the other side.

Blending The Cap

To trim the edge of the cap, use a pair of scissors after pulling the cap up and out of the adhesive. Cut away the excess cap and lay the newly trimmed edge back down into the adhesive. Do this all the way around the cap. The chemical that is used to dissolve the vinyl is acetone. Acetone is highly volatile, which means it evaporates very quickly. Use a cotton swab and lightly dab it onto the edge. Take precautions to protect the eyes from the acetone, place a powder puff over the eyes so nothing can drip down into them. Keep in mind there should not be an excess of acetone to drip, use it sparingly. An additional way to get the edge to blend is to apply something that will build the skin up to the same level as the surface of the cap. Apply ridge filler to the skin and blend it into the cap. It is very important to keep the ridge filler off the cap, because if it is applied to both the skin and the cap it will not actually fix anything, instead the edge would just get bigger. The ridge filler is used to fill in the edge created by the cap as it sits on top of the skin. Use a pallet knife to apply it, starting on the skin and sweeping it up to the edge of the cap without going over. Apply the ridge filler all the way around the cap. To match the texture of the cap to the skin, apply two or three layers of plastic sealer over the edge of the cap and onto the skin.

Coloring The Cap

This step of the application is the most critical. If a mistake is made here, even if the application is perfect, the cap may not turn out well. However if mistakes are made during the application of the cap, this step could completely save it. First, mix a perfect base match using regular cream make-up. It is very important to mix the right base color, because it is the base for the entire make-up. Using a pallet knife spread the base color onto the cap; a little will go a long way. With a white sponge, stipple the color together, blending and moving it over the head. Use a large brush that is damp with 99% alcohol to blend the edge of the color into the skin. Powder the base with a liberal amount of pigmented powder. With a brush, apply shading and highlight colors to the cap. It is okay to go a little darker than normal, because more base colors will be applied over the highlight and shadow. Paint the shadow under the jawbone, beneath the cheekbone, into the temples and onto the forehead. Wherever possible apply the shadow across the edge of the cap; this will help to further blend the edge. The highlight should be placed on top of the cheekbones and along the bone structure that makes up the eye sockets. Powder the highlights and shadows. With an orange stipple sponge, stipple at least three different shades of base color onto the cap, one lighter, another darker, and a base match, which will give the cap its needed texture. This will also help soften the highlights and shadows, and of course help blend the edge. Using the orange stipple sponge, apply small amounts of both blue and green mixed with the base color. This will give the bald cap that translucent skin quality. A small amount of mustard yellow may be needed to help the colors blend. Finally, apply a brick color to the cap to give it the necessary redness of skin; do not be afraid to use a lot. Both film and television will remove a little of the red, so it is desirable to use slightly more than what seems to be right. Lightly powder the cap when finished with a translucent powder.

Student Dalton Kutsch
Year   2007

Student Patricia Moja
Year   2005

Student Meg Brown
Year   2006

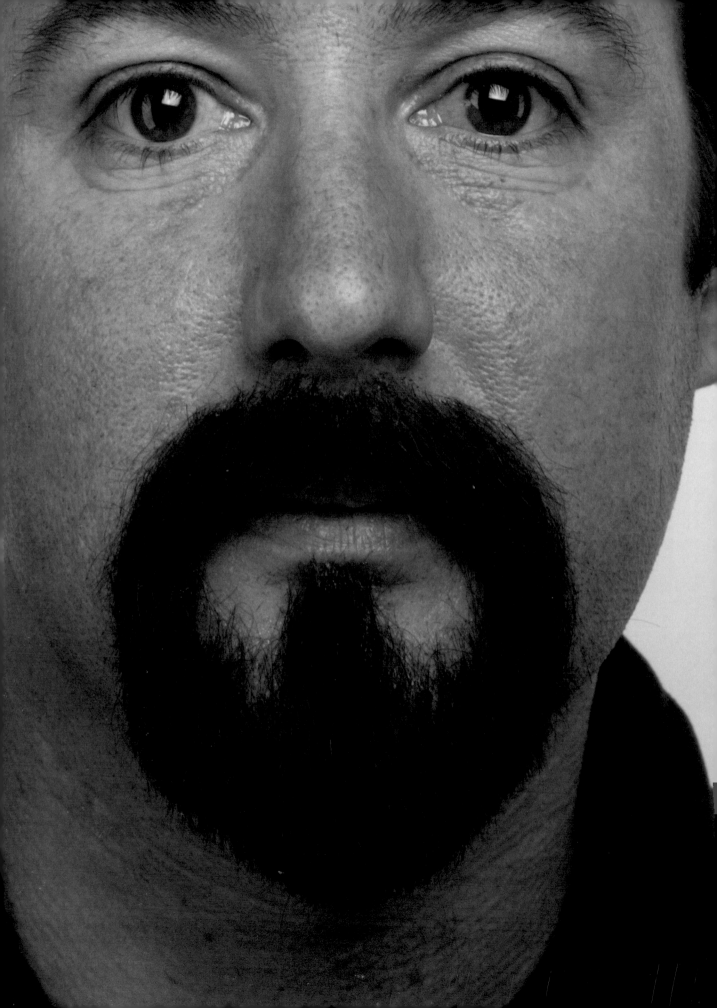

CHAPTER 11

Beards & Mustaches

Facial hair varies from individual to individual as well as ethnic groups. For example, men from many Asian and African backgrounds typically have much less facial hair than those of European, Middle Eastern, and South Asian descent. In addition, Native Americans typically have little to no facial hair at all. A beard specifically refers to the facial hair on the lower part of the chin, while the moustache refers to hair above the upper lip and around it. The make-up artist must research the style and period of the character's beard or mustache before designing one.

Applying hair is not particularly difficult but requires practice and an understanding of how the different pieces of hair are going to fit together. Like a puzzle, there should be no gaps between each section and each piece must to be cut to fit. One aspect that must always be considered is the density of hair - how many individual strands are within a square inch. Facial hair, depending on the character, should be evenly placed with a small amount of skin showing through. The hair at the edge of the beard, such as on the cheek, should be less dense. Creating an even application with complete coverage of the area with skin showing through is the trick to a realistic beard.

Several types of hair can be used for beard application depending on budget and the length required for the character. There is human hair, yak hair, crepe wool, and synthetic hair. The most commonly used are human and yak and most human hair comes from Asia. Hair is often categorized as Asian or European; however European hair is usually from India. Asian hair is the most readily available and it is slightly coarser than Western hair. Human hair comes in a multitude of categories and is priced accordingly. For a beard application most human hair will work without having to worry about the different qualities. The two major differences in quality are "remy" and "non-remy" hair. Remy hair is bundled in such a manner that the roots are on one side and the tips are on the other. Since all the hairs lie in the same direction, they are undisturbed, making them more durable and less likely to tangle. Non-remy hair has the root and the tip mixed. Yak hair is very similar to human hair and is most commonly used in extensions as a lower priced option. Crepe wool is not hair at all; it is wool in long strands that simulate hair

and is mainly used in the theater and for learning purposes due to its low cost. Synthetic hair is made of a wide array of synthetic fibers. The quality varies greatly but, if well maintained, synthetic hair can look as good as the real thing. It is also much less expensive and often used in situations where a long beard is required.

For most projects a combination of human and yak hair are mixed together to create a realistic look. Both are sold in ten to twelve inch lengths, either on a weft, or as a pre-crimped bundle. The pre-crimped bundles are ready to be mixed and used by the make-up artist. If purchasing hair on a weft, it will need to be prepared prior to application. The hair will need to be cut away from the weft and crimped to simulate facial hair. Crepe wool comes in a variety of colors, none of which are very realistic on their own, but can be mixed together to produce a more realistic look. Crepe wool is about six to eight inches in length and a braided yard will usually yield enough hair to do several beards. For synthetic hair, there is very little preparation required. It is purchased either straight or crimped and it is ready for use. There is no cuticle layer to worry about and it comes in a variety of lengths. Synthetic hair is usually attached to lace and can be somewhat more difficult to apply as a hand-laid beard.

There are two main methods of application; loose hair applied by hand or the application of a ventilated lace hairpiece. A lace hairpiece is the fastest way to get hair glued to the face, but it is less comfortable and more costly to make than a hand-laid beard. Hand laying hair is time consuming and difficult to match for continuity on a daily basis, whereas a lace beard can be reapplied multiple times and will match perfectly. Keep in mind that even if lace hairpieces are used, the edge of the beard will still need to be hand-laid for the most realistic look.

One element to achieving this is to match the false hair to the performers' natural hair color. In some cases they will match perfectly and in others it may be lighter or darker. To properly match color it is best to identify two or three colors that are present on the performer. Later, using false hair, blend those colors together to create a similar mixture of hair. For example, the performer's hair is blonde, and the individual colors that make up that person's hair color is mostly a light blonde with a few strands of light and dark brown and a small percentage of gray. The artist would blend together seventy-five percent light blond, ten percent light brown, ten percent dark brown, and five percent gray. The proper way to blend is to hold a mixed handful at one end and pull the hair out at the other end. The hair will separate causing the individual strands to mix with the others. Repeat the process until a uniform color is achieved. Be sure to blend enough for the length of the project. The hair will need to be hackled once the blending is complete. A hackle is a piece of wood or metal with a series of closely placed pins, set-up in rows that are used like a giant comb to detangle hair. As hair is run through the hackle, short hairs and tangles will build up in the pins; when this happens the hair must be removed and set aside. The short left over pieces of hair can be hackled separately and sorted into piles of different lengths.

There are many choices of adhesives, the most common are silicone and spirit gum. Spirit gum has been used since the early days of film and continues to be a good choice for gluing on hair. Depending on the manufacturer, spirit gum may need a matting agent. For example TS-100 matting agent helps remove some of the shine from the adhesive. Spirit gum also requires the extra step of tapping the glue to make it tacky just prior to applying the hair. Silicone adhesives are more common now due to ease of use. They are used in conjunction with a matching thinner that allows the adhesive to be thinned or reactivated.

Before starting a beard, the direction of the hair growth and the style of the beard need to be considered. The growth pattern of facial hair varies from individual to individual and needs to be decided upon prior to application. In most cases, hair on the neck and below the chin grows in a forward direction. Hair on the chin and mustache area grows in a downward direction and angles slightly away from center. Hair from the cheeks down to the jaw line grows toward the jaw line, and hair at the side burns angle back towards the ears. Following this pattern is ideal as long as the beard is fairly short in length. For longer beards, hair is usually applied in a downward direction due to the weight. Some styles of long beards have the hair directed toward the chin and the hair is applied to facilitate this type of look. Knowing the final style and direction of the hair dictates how it will be applied.

Preparation Of Crepe Wool

The following is a step-by-step procedure for properly preparing crepe wool. Only crepe wool needs this procedure as all the other available hairs can be purchased already prepared. For the purpose of learning how to apply hair, crepe wool is an inexpensive alternative to using human or yak hair.

This is the crepe wool as it comes from the package. This type of hair is not really hair at all; it is actually wool woven into a braid.

Step 1

To prepare crepe wool for use it must first be unraveled from the strings. Lightly pull on one end of a braid; the wool will separate slightly from the strings. Now, unravel the strings away from the wool. The hair and strings will become knotted if pulled too hard or far.

Step 2

To keep the hair and strings from knotting as they are pulled, simply cut off the excess strings. Continue until the strings are completely removed from the braid. Once the strings have been removed eliminate approximately sixty percent of the curl from the wool. More can be removed, but this may result in a very flat look.

Step 3

Simply hang the wool strand over a steady stream of steam; the wool will slowly relax as it is held there. Be careful not to leave it too long or the hair will completely straighten.

Straighter crepe wool is easier to apply; unfortunately it is less realistic as well. One notable exception is Asian facial hair. This type of hair tends to be very straight requiring almost all of the curl to be removed before application. Another exception is the application of African-American facial hair.

Step 5

Once the end is straightened, grab the end of the wool and hold it in the stream of steam. As it straightens, move the wool along the opening of the steamer, slowly relaxing the curl of the entire braid. Do not stretch the wool braid as it is held.

The wool after it is steamed.

Step 6

Pull the straightened braid of crepe wool apart. Hold the wool from one end and gently begin pulling from the other. The wool fibers will separate into six to eight inch pieces.

Step 7

Once all the hair is separated, then finish preparing it by continuing to pull from the ends.

Step 8

Hold the hair at one end with a good grip then pull from the other. This will further separate the individual strands of wool, enhancing the look of the hair. Return the hair to the bundle then pull it again. Repeat this procedure until the wool looks fluffy and even.

Step 9

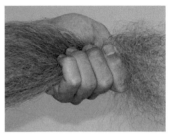

A close-up of the hair being held: the forefinger and thumb are holding the bulk of the hair. If the hair is gripped too tightly it will not pull apart properly.

The finished hair is piled up then wrapped in a paper towel for safekeeping.

The Hackle And Its Use

A hackle is a piece of wood or metal with a series of closely placed pins, set up in rows, that are used like a giant comb to de-tangle most types of hair.

Step 1

The hackle should be clamped or taped securely to the edge of the counter. When not in use always cover the hackle with a piece of balsa wood, a tissue box, or anything that will prevent injury.

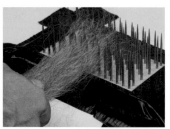

Step 2

Hair is run through the hackle to remove short hairs and tangles from the pile of hair being prepared.

Step 3

Hold onto the center of the hair with a good grip; do not let the hair escape between fingers as it is detangled.

Step 4

To properly use the hackle, begin by carefully placing approximately an inch handful of hair into the hackle. Do this very carefully and slowly, as the pins in the hackle are quite sharp. Holding the hair firmly and pull it through the hackle.

Step 5

Move fingers down an inch then run the hair through the hackle until the center of the chunk of hair is reached. Turn the hair around and repeat the entire process again with the other half of the hair.

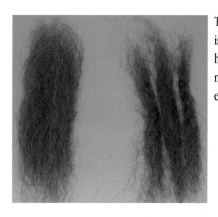

The hair on the left is hackled, but the hair on the right is not. Hackled hair is easier to apply.

Continue until all of the hair needed has been run through the hackle. As it is run through the hackle, short hairs and tangles will build up in the pins. When the short hairs and tangles begin to interfere with the hair being prepared they should be removed and set aside. Take the short hair and tangled pieces and pull them apart end from end, until the hair is straightened out and can be run through the hackle. You may repeat this procedure until all of the hair has been straightened and separated into piles of different lengths. Never throw away any of the hair that is left behind in the hackle. Even the left over fuzz can be used for beard stubble.

Proper Cutting Technique

Applying hair breaks down into a few simple steps. Properly cutting the hair is key to a good application.

Step 1

Grip the hair properly; hold it tightly between the thumb and forefinger. Once the process is started do not let go until the hair is placed on the face.

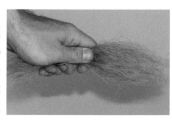

Step 2

To get the hair to flair out properly, comb it against a leg.

Step 3

Hold the hair in the position it is to be applied; visualizing the shape it will have once placed.

Step 4

Cut the top edge off the hair. The shape is not important, round, square, or triangular, any will do.

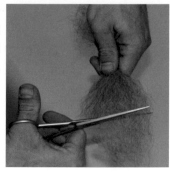

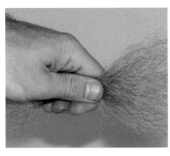

The amount of hair sticking out from the fingers will directly relate to how thick the hair is applied. The further back the hair is held the thinner the application, while the closer to the end the hair is held the thicker it will be.

Step 6

Cut each side of the piece to control the amount of stray hairs.

Step 7

Notice how we turn the hair, so when it is cut the shavings fall away without getting stuck in the piece.

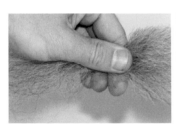

Step 8

The hair is now ready to be beveled.

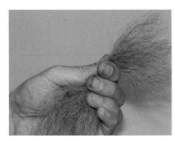

Step 9

Turn the hair sideways holding it in the direction in which it will grow; in this case a downward direction.

Step 10

Next, hold the scissors parallel to the face as the backside of the hair is cut. This is called beveling.

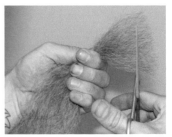

Step 11

Make sure all the cuttings fall away from the piece that is going to be applied.

The finished bevel cut ready to be applied

Hand Laid Hair

The art form of hand laying hair to a performer's face is slowly being forgotten. Many make-up artists feel the process is completely different from any other type of make-up they may be asked to do. Some even think this should be the job of the hairdresser. As the make-up artist, we are responsible for the total look of the actor.

Typically, hand-laying hair is not used in most productions because of the difficulty in matching it on a daily basis. Continuity is such a large concern that it has led to the use of pre-made lace appliances for most productions. However, because hand-laying hair is relatively inexpensive it is still utilized for background performers and low budget projects. Keeping the station and tools clean and organized is a huge part of a successful application.

A couple of suggestions – do not use too much hair and remember the hair should essentially stand on end, with only the ends of the hair stuck in the glue.

Step 1

We will be using crepe wool for this beard. As previously discussed, the wool comes in predetermined lengths of about six to eight inches. Take a small amount to start with and make sure to comb through it thoroughly before using the hair.

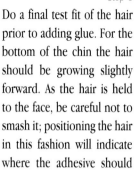

Step 5

Do a final test fit of the hair prior to adding glue. For the bottom of the chin the hair should be growing slightly forward. As the hair is held to the face, be careful not to smash it; positioning the hair in this fashion will indicate where the adhesive should be applied.

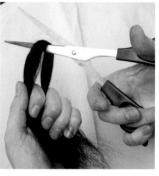

Step 2

Fold the hair in half making a loop and then cut it on the top of loop. Because the hair is not a uniform length, most of the hair would fall out if it were applied without cutting first. We are cutting it in half because we are going to make a short beard.

Step 6

Dip a cotton swab into the silicone thinner and then into the silicone adhesive; this will help keep the adhesive thin as it goes on the skin. The brand of adhesive chosen will depend on how much working time is needed to stick the hair to the face.

Step 3

Trim the first piece of hair for the bottom of the chin. Notice how the hair is held; the index finger is wrapped around the hair and the thumb is pressed firmly to the finger, holding the hair in a very tight fashion. Once the hair is in this position do not let go until it is stuck to the face or it will have to be trimmed again.

Step 7

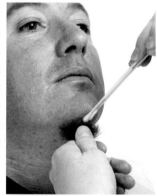

Once the area is coated in glue, gently press the hair into it and hold until dry. The nice thing about silicone adhesives is their ability to dry quickly. Use the back of the wooden cotton swab to press the hair into the adhesive.

Step 8

Once the adhesive is dry and the hair stuck to the face relax the death grip on the hair. Carefully pick through the hair to remove any that is not stuck in the adhesive.

Step 4

Hold the hair to the chin to measure and see what needs to be trimmed. Cut away all unwanted hair and be sure to bevel the remainder that is going to stick to the face.

Notice the thinness of the hair left on the chin. This is perfect, additional hair will be added in front of this piece and it is necessary to see into the hair. If the hair gets too thick the beard will look fake.

Press the hair into the glue and use the cotton swab to stick down any hair that is not touching the adhesive. Comb through it in the same fashion as the others.

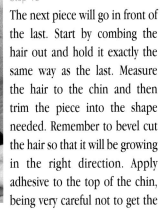

The next piece will go in front of the last. Start by combing the hair out and hold it exactly the same way as the last. Measure the hair to the chin and then trim the piece into the shape needed. Remember to bevel cut the hair so that it will be growing in the right direction. Apply adhesive to the top of the chin, being very careful not to get the glue in the first piece of hair.

In this photograph we are illustrating how to properly measure a piece. We hold the hair in the direction of the hair growth and we are holding the scissors to show how much hair we will have to cut off.

Press the hair into the glue as soon as the adhesive is applied. The hair should look like it is growing out of the skin, so carefully lay the edges into the adhesive. Again, use the pick side of a comb to gently remove the stray hairs.

This piece was adhered following the same process we have been talking about with each application. Stay neat and clean and perfect in the process; comb, measure, cut, bevel, apply the hair, and remove strays to create amazing beards.

Next is the small piece that goes under the lower lip. We have combed, measured, trimmed, and beveled this piece in the exact same way as the last, using a little less adhesive than the previous piece.

The mustache is done in the same way as the rest of the beard, only in smaller pieces. Notice that we are holding the hair in a tighter fashion and the ends are closer to the fingers. Start where the beard stops; there should not be any gap between them.

Step 17

Start by the corners of the mouth and work inward. Apply a piece on the right side then on the left, moving from side to side for each piece. This will allow for a more even application.

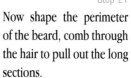

Step 21

Now shape the perimeter of the beard, comb through the hair to pull out the long sections.

Step 18

Work until the hair meets in the middle under the nose. Working in this area can be a problem for the performer so take special care not to tickle the nose with excess hair.

Step 22

Keeping the scissors parallel to the area that is being cut will prevent taking out a chunk of the beard accidentally.

Step 23

Use tweezers to remove any stray hairs from the beard and from the surface of the skin. We recommend tweezing between every piece applied.

Step 19

Now that the hair is all applied it must be trimmed into a normal beard. Start with the mustache and trim the hair back to the upper lip. Only trim the center–most part, making sure not to cut the sides over the corners of the mouth.

Step 20

To cut the sides over the corners of the mouth, hold the scissors almost parallel to the skin, trimming in a downward motion.

The finished beard; note how skin is showing through the hair.

Floating A Beard

The phrase "floating a beard" refers to the process of removing a beard from a Tuffie head. The beard may also be called a plastic beard. The reason for this is because there is no lace used in this type of appliance, only a plastic spray.

Hair is applied to a Tuffie head with either spirit gum or a silicone adhesive, and typically in the shape of a beard, but just about any shape can be done. The hair is trimmed to a desired length and dressed accordingly with curling irons.

The beard is sprayed with a clear acrylic coating from a distance of twelve to fifteen inches. After ten minutes, remove the beard with a cotton swab dipped in acetone. Apply the acetone to the Tuffie head immediately above the upper hairline. As the acetone runs between the block and the beard, it will dissolve the adhesive and release the beard. It is a slow process of carefully dripping the acetone down the front of the Tuffie head, but with a little patience the beard will be totally removed. Keep in mind, when removing a beard from a person, 99% alcohol should be used instead of the acetone; it will take a little longer but will be much safer and gentler for the performer. Once the beard is removed from the form, spray more acrylic coating to the back of it. The beard is now ready to be applied to a performer. It can be re-used over and over as long as special care is used in removing it each time.

Tuffie Head Beard

This is an example of a full beard on a Tuffie head. This beard could be done exactly the same way on a performer or can be removed from the Tuffie head in the same fashion as described in Floating a Beard.

The photograph depicts a hackle, wig clamp, and Tuffie head typically used to practice hand-laid hair work, or "float" facial hair pieces, previously built upon the form.

Spirit gum adhesive is applied to the bottom of the chin. After the glue has been tapped, gently press the hair into the adhesive. The brush is used to guide the hair into place.

The top of the chin is painted with spirit gum. After the adhesive has been tapped, press the hair into it. The grip on the hair is relaxed as the brush is used to guide the hair into position.

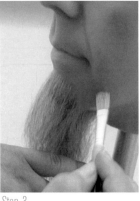

Step 3

After the adhesive has been properly applied to the face, position the hair according to the desired growth direction. Press the hair into place.

Step 4

Hair is applied to both sides of the face to maintain balance and symmetry. Observe the desired growth direction when pressing the hair into the adhesive.

Step 5

Hair is applied to the upper beard area and sideburn. The growth direction is established; hair is applied growing slightly backward.

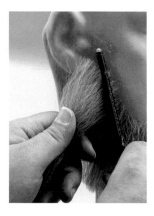

Step 6

Hair is applied to the opposite side of the face in the same pattern.

Step 7

Hair is applied to both sides of the face, completing the sideburn and making a transition into the performer's growth direction.

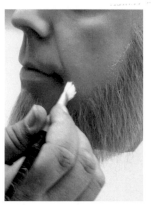

Step 8

Hair is applied near the corners of the mouth creating the lower portion of the mustache. The growth direction is slightly outward and the hair down close to the skin.

Step 9

Continue to apply hair above the corners of the mouth and just inside of the nasolabial fold. Observe the natural beard pattern of the model or use photographic reference.

Step 11

Gently press the hair into the philtrum, or cupid's bow. Use a brush handle or comb to secure the hair and establish the growth direction.

Step 10

Hair is applied on each side, moving toward the center. The mustache begins to shift growth direction, becoming straighter as the application approaches the center.

Step 12

Hair is applied to complete the mustache. The growth direction should reflect a straight out and downward movement. The mustache is trimmed according to desired style and transitioned into the beard work. The mustache can be styled with a light mist of water that will weigh down any loose hairs. Set the style of the mustache with a firm-hold hairspray, or clear acrylic spray.

The completed beard work reflects the length and style desired to establish the film or television character.

Lace Piece Ventilating

Ventilating is the process of hand knotting individual hairs to a piece of lace. This is done to simulate a beard, mustache, or hair growth. The lace is cut and trimmed into a desired shape and hair is then hand knotted to it, creating a re-usable hair appliance. Human, yak, and synthetic hair are commonly used in this type of lace appliance. The only limitation with synthetic hair is it cannot be curled with the Marcel iron and oven.

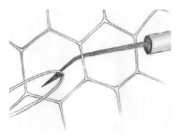

Step 1

The first step is to push the needle through a hole and then back out through another hole in the lace. Hook a single strand of hair with the needle.

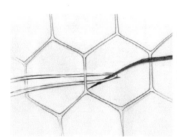

Step 2

Turn the needle sideways and pull the single strand of hair through the lace.

Step 3

Push the needle forward once it clears the lace. The needle is still looped by the hair.

Step 4

Push the needle through until it is close to the hair that has not passed through the lace.

Step 5

Then hook the strand of hair that has not passed through the lace.

Step 6

Spin the needle, wrapping the end of the strand around it.

Step 7

Then pull through the loop.

Step 8

The completed knot of hair.

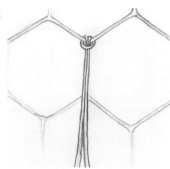

Dressing A Lace Beard

Before applying a lace beard to the performer it typically needs to be dressed, which means the beard needs to be trimmed and curled to give it a more natural appearance. A lace beard can be used multiple times and will need to be curled daily.

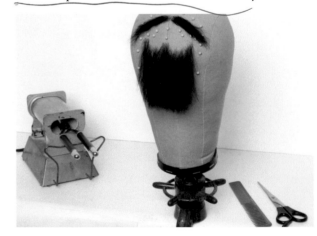

Shown is the beard and mustache properly pinned to a wig block. Even though the hair is wavy it still needs to be curled to give the beard body. The tools needed for this process are a comb, scissors, and a small Marcel curling iron and oven.

Step 1

Test the iron on a piece of tissue to make sure it is not too hot for the hair. If it is too hot it will leave a burn mark on the tissue, and if it is too cool it will not curl the hair.

Step 2

Separate the mustache into smaller sections to allow for easy access of individual sections. Each section of hair will need to be curled towards the lip.

Step 3

Curl the section close to the lace without touching it. By curling it close to the lace, the hair will look like it is growing out of the skin.

Step 4

Trim the excess hair to finish grooming the mustache.

Step 5

The beard is separated in the same way as the mustache. It will be separated from top to bottom as well as left to right.

Step 6

Again, work close to the lace without touching it and make sure enough curl is created.

Step 7

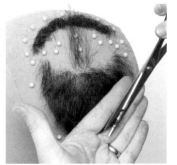

Trim any excessively long hairs; hold hair between fingers as a guide to keep the beard uniform.

Step 8

At any point more curl can be added if necessary.

Step 9

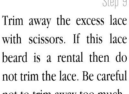

Trim away the excess lace with scissors. If this lace beard is a rental then do not trim the lace. Be careful not to trim away too much.

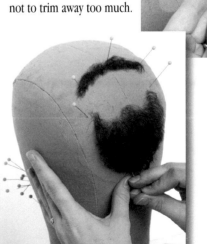

This is the finished beard and mustache ready to be applied to the performer.

Applying A Lace Beard

The best part about using a lace beard is its ease and speed of application. Being able to reuse it over and over is also a benefit. The end result is the same with every beard we do; the performer should look like they have a beard. We have chosen the same performer to show the difference between a hand-laid and pre-made beard on lace.

Step 1

Test fit the beard to the performer to make sure it is going to fit the face.

Step 2

Apply silicone adhesive to the center of the chin area. The application of adhesive for a lace appliance is very similar to a prosthetic appliance. Spirit gum could also be used for a lace application.

Step 3

Press the beard into the adhesive, being careful not to stick the hair into it. Stretch the beard into position.

Step 4

Pull back on the unglued area and apply more adhesive; apply only enough to cover the area that is to be adhered.

Step 5

Press the lace into the new adhesive area while turning a cotton swab around to lightly tap the edges of lace into the adhesive.

Step 6

The same procedure is used on each side of the beard. Remember to stretch the lace lightly to ensure a good fit. Also, have the performer hold open his mouth slightly to stretch the area being adhered.

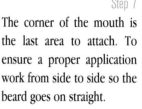

Step 7

The corner of the mouth is the last area to attach. To ensure a proper application work from side to side so the beard goes on straight.

Step 8

Test-fit the mustache to the upper lip and note how it will fit to the beard.

Step 9

Apply adhesive in the center of the lip area, just enough to give a good adhesion point and to allow for adjustment of the position of the mustache.

Lift up on the mustache and apply adhesive right next to the last adhesive spot. Then lay the lace into the tacky adhesive. Remember to work on both sides of the mustache, alternating from one side to the other to ensure a straight application.

Step 11

Lift up on the corner of the mustache to apply more adhesive; it may be necessary for the performer to open his mouth again to allow the lace to lie down in the adhesive.

Step 12

If any of the hair has gone a little flat it may be necessary to re-curl. Use a metal comb to protect the performer from the hot iron and curl the hair the same way as when it was dressed.

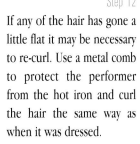

Step 13

Mustache wax can be used to help the hair keep its curl and shape. Apply a little to a pallet and work it into a make-up brush.

Step 14

Apply the wax over the hair with a brush or your fingers. If the hair were a little longer it could be shaped with the wax.

The finished lace beard applied to the performer.

CHAPTER 12

Bruises

Bruise Progression

Bruises are one of the most common types of special make-up effects done by the make-up artist they are also open to a wide variety of interpretations. Since every person bruises a little differently, we have found bruising to be highly subjective. So what we will be talking about in this section is the typical and the norm. Remember, every time a bruise is created it will be somewhat different with each interpretation.

Step 1

Stipple a mixture of red and maroon creating the effect of broken capillaries.

Typical Station set-up for minor injuries

Step 2

Stipple the dark red color on the area where the bruise will be created. Apply the color lightly and allow the skin to show through the color.

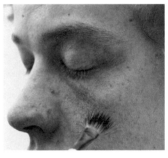

To do bruises properly the artist must first understand why skin bruises and what causes all the different colors. A bruise is caused by internal bleeding when the skin is hit hard enough for the capillaries in it to break. Redness shows first and then as the blood begins to coagulate it will turn maroon. The blood will darken becoming more blue/purple and in some cases black. As the bruise begins to "heal," the areas with the highest concentration of blood will turn a brownish/bluish color, while the area immediately around the dark patches of skin becomes yellow.

Step 3

The principals of highlight and shadow are present in every form of make-up, even in a bruise.

Fresh Bruise

To create a bruise with make-up is relatively simple. Subtlety is everything when creating a bruise. Some artists prefer using a flat brush, smashed to flare all the hairs out. An orange or a black stipple sponge can be used, however these seem to leave a very even pattern on the skin. Spread a dark red color onto a pallet, so the brush will pick up the color evenly.

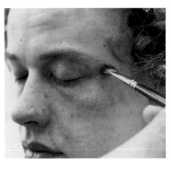

Step 4

Use the maroon as a shadow, and stipple it over the dark red. This will create areas of swelling and also simulate the most damaged areas with blood.

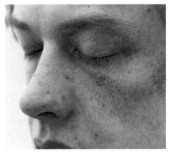

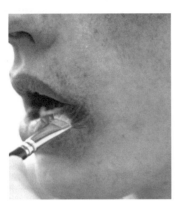

Step 5

The same steps can be applied to any area, such as the corner of the mouth.

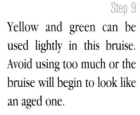

Step 9

Yellow and green can be used lightly in this bruise. Avoid using too much or the bruise will begin to look like an aged one.

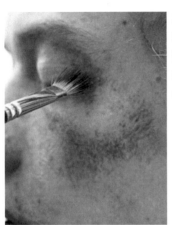

Step 6

Stipple a small amount of blue/purple onto the maroon to deepen the shadows slightly.

Step 7

The natural skin color is used as the highlight. However, the skin is usually red all over, so leaving it untouched may appear odd.

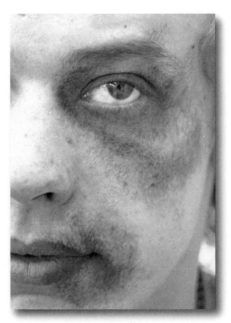

The finished effect

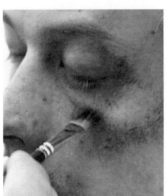

Step 8

A light red stain can be applied to the highlights to give the skin area color. Do not darken the area too much.

Bruise, Using Alcohol-Based Make-up

Alcohol-based make-up comes in a variety of forms and colors. Unlike traditional cream make-up, this type is designed to be durable and does not require the use of powders to set the product. Several companies produce colors that are developed to imitate the natural coloration of wounds and injuries. The resulting injuries, painted with alcohol-based products, achieve the depth and intensity of real life wounds. With much of the guesswork removed, an artist can feel confident in their ability to maintain continuity, and trust in the resiliency of an alcohol-based make-up.

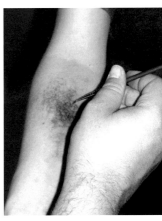

Step 4

A translucent wash of a blue tone is stippled into select areas of purple and red. Blue also adds depth and replicates the tones apparent in severe bruising.

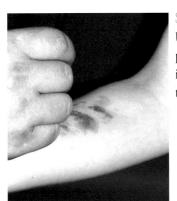

Step 1

Using a textured brush, stipple concentrations of an irregular bright red tone onto the skin.

The completed bruise using alcohol-based make-up is sealed

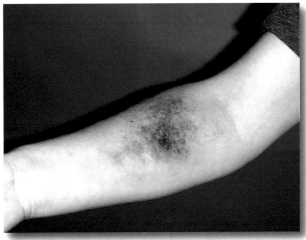

with a plastic fixative spray. After sealing, the artist may increase the level of shine with a water-based lubricant like KY jelly.

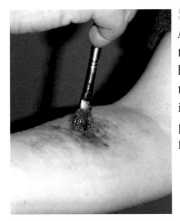

Step 2

Apply maroon and purple tones, texturing each into the bright red. Allow each color to be translucent, and build intensity by concentrating pigments in an overlapping fashion.

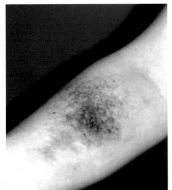

Step 3

Increase the depth and intensity of the purple tones using a smaller brush. The purple adds contrast to the overall look of the bruise.

Aged Bruise

To create a healing or aged bruise we use the same technique as a new one, however the colors will be a little different. An old bruise consists more of dried blood under the skin with a faint hint of yellow around it.

Step 1
Stipple on a yellowish/green color in an uneven pattern. The yellow/green should be used the same way the dark red color was applied. Allow the skin to show through the make-up.

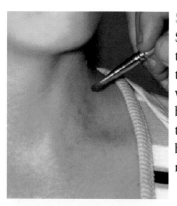

Step 2
Stipple brownish/blue over the yellow/green in the areas that are most damaged and which would have the most blood. Do not shadow with the dark color because the bruise is healing and would no longer be swollen.

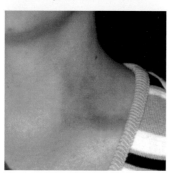

Step 3
Use a teal professional pencil to add a faint blue/green color often found in healing bruises.

Scrapes And Scratches

The following is a very simple effect created with color to give the illusion of depth. Scrapes and scratches can be achieved with wax or as a prosthetic, but in this case we will use color. Drag a dark red color across the skin in a straight line with a black stipple sponge. The lines created by the sponge should taper off in both directions. With a thin brush, paint on very thin black lines over the dark red color and taper the ends of the lines. Draw additional

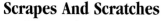

lines into the dark red color making them various lengths and in different areas. Remember to keep the lines of red and black running in the same direction as each other. Finally, add a small amount of liquid blood to each of the black lines.

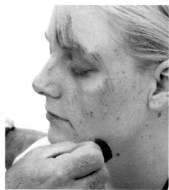

Step 1
Use a coarse black stipple sponge and a combination of two red colors to create a deep blood red. Drag the dark red color across the face in even straight movement. Try to keep the red lines intense in some areas and lighter in others.

Step 2
Remember to keep the scrape going in one direction. Use a clean side of the sponge and drag in the opposite direction. This will keep little dots of red from forming where the scrape was started.

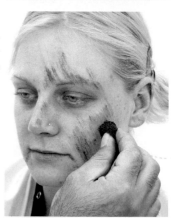

Step 3
Use a maroon to deepen a few of the areas. The darker color helps to add a look of irritation. Do not cover the entire area with the maroon color; only add it in small amounts while dragging the color the same direction as the red.

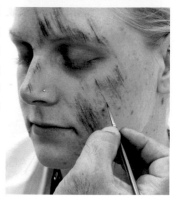

Step 4
With a small brush, paint ultra thin black lines into the most injured looking areas of the red. The black lines will represent the small cuts in the skin.

Step 5

Fake Blood is applied over each black line and over some of the red ones to finish the effect.

Step 1

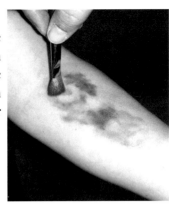

Using a brush, apply bruise powder to the skin in an irregular pattern. Allow the powder to concentrate in some areas and remain sheer in others.

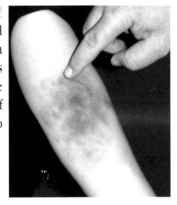

Step 2

After establishing the general area of the bruise, use a clean fingertip to rub across the bruise powder. The rubbing and compression of the product will cause it to change to shades of purple.

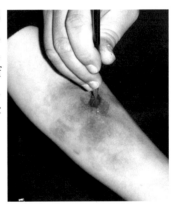

Step 3

Using a brush and 99% alcohol, texture the bruised area. Notice how small pockets of skin are allowed to be visible. This technique creates realistic bruise textures.

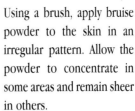

The finished look of the scrape.

Bruise Powder

Bruise powder is a product produced by Principality Medical in the United Kingdom, and distributed at several vendors in the United States. This powder appears to be packaged as dry pigment, however after applying it to clean skin it changes color to tones of purples and reds.

Bruise powder becomes an invaluable product in situations where many different bruises need to be applied, or when large portions of the body need to be bruised quickly. Loose powders are difficult to control, and in situations where continuity may be required, a bruise will prove difficult to replicate. Bruise powder is truly advantageous when continuity maintenance is not required.

Step 4

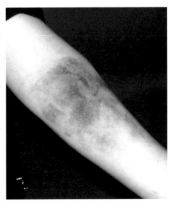

The completed bruise application is sealed with a plastic fixative spray. After sealing, the artist may increase the level of shine with a water-based lubricant like KY jelly.

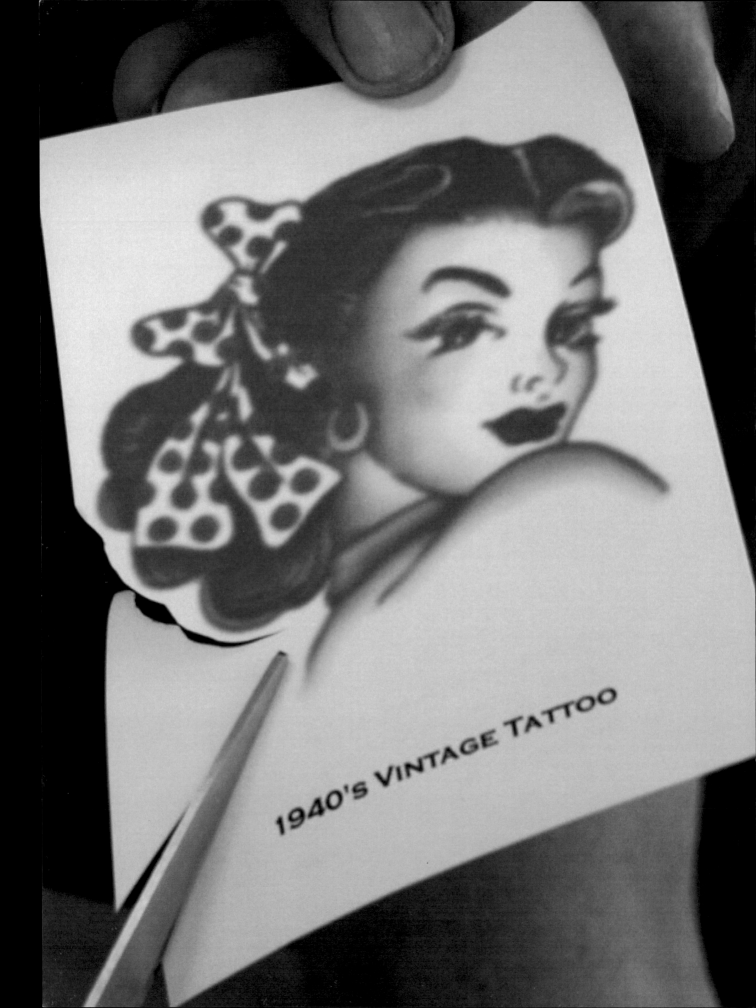

CHAPTER 13

Tattoos

Tattoos are a fairly easy proposition, even if there is no formal background in drawing, there are several ways to approach them. The simplest tattoo is the sticker style, while the freehand drawing is the hardest one to do and match on a daily basis. Most tattoos purchased at a make-up supplier will come with a complete set of instructions.

Freehand Drawn Tattoo

The most difficult thing to accomplish and match on a daily basis is a freehand drawn tattoo on the actor. Using a taupe make-up pencil, sketch the tattoo as desired. A black make-up pencil is used to finalize the design into a tattoo, followed by the use of a teal professional pencil over the black to create the aged look. The same effect can be achieved with alcohol-based make-up made by many manufacturers. The make-up can also be used to color the tattoo. The advantage of the alcohol-based make-up is that it is dry and will not rub off until removed with alcohol. Powder the tattoo completely with a pigmented powder to finish. The next series of photographs illustrate how to sketch out a design and then darken it. This is slow because it is necessary to go over the design three times. KD 151's tattoo pens can be used to complete the tattoo. Use a taupe pencil to sketch out the design and then use KD 151's aged ink pencil in either 50% or 75% to create the aged look of a tattoo; this will work better than using black and teal pencils. An added bonus is that the tattoo pens will not rub off.

Step 2

Shade with the pencil and wrap up the design

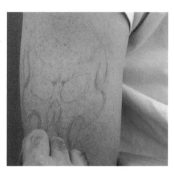

Step 3

The finished design

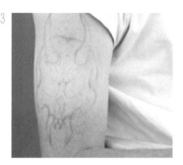

Step 4

Add black with a make-up pencil. Use the black to finalize the shape.

Step 1

Lightly sketch the design with a taupe make-up pencil, slowly adding in elements.

Step 5

Darken in the eyes and nose. Darken remaining shadows and add details.

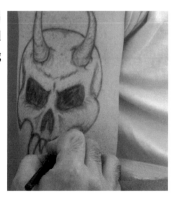

Step 6

Clean off any taupe lines not being used with a cotton swab and 99% alcohol.

Step 7

Use the teal make-up pencil to age the lines.

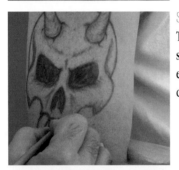

Step 8

The teal is used on the shadows to soften the edges, as well as to age the color.

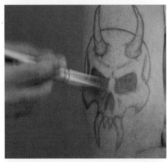

Step 9

Powder the pencil lines. Dust off the excess powder.

Step 10

Completed freehand drawn tattoo.

Water Slide Tattoo

A plastic transfer style tattoo is very similar to a sticker. These types of tattoo can be purchased from a local make-up supplier in the form of a predetermined design. Several of the companies making tattoos can custom make them to fit the needs of a project. The nice thing about these types of tattoos is their ease of application and once applied there is no need to color them. Continuity on this type of tattoo is very simple. It is applied with water and removed with any oil based make-up remover. These tattoos are usually full color and come in a wide variety of shapes and sizes. They may look shiny when applied; to control the shine use a small amount of powder or mortician's wax. Simply use a finger to pat the wax over the surface of the sticker.

Examples of an off-the-shelf style tattoo made by Tinsley Tattoos.

Step 1

Trim as close to the tattoo as possible with a pair of scissors.

Step 2

Trimming around the tattoo allows it to easily conform to the area it is being applied. Next, remove the protective plastic cover off the front of the tattoo.

Step 3

Apply to a clean and dry surface. Press firmly to the skin and hold.

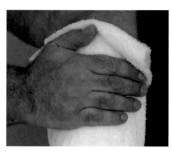

Press a damp towel to the back of the tattoo and hold there for several seconds. Allow the water to penetrate the paper backing and soak through to the tattoo.

Alcohol Transfer Tattoo

A good alternative to both these types of tattoos is the alcohol transfer tattoo. There are several companies manufacturing these types of tattoos and again most are found at any make-up supplier. Another way to create a transfer tattoo is to have someone design it on paper or copy an existing piece of artwork. Photocopy the artwork several times to make multiple tattoo transfers. Turn the artwork upside down on a light box and trace the image with an inkblot pencil called "A Bottle of Ink in a Pencil" onto newsprint paper. The paper is then applied in the same fashion except that to transfer it to the skin you would use water instead of alcohol. This pencil is available in most art and make-up supply stores and can be used directly on the skin with water. The transfer tattoo is not designed as a standalone application. In both cases it requires either make-up pencils, alcohol-based make-up or tattoo pens.

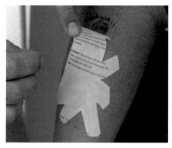

Step 5

Once the tattoo is sufficiently wet, slowly peel the paper away.

Step 6

Carefully peel the paper without removing the tattoo.

Step 1

Cut as close to the tattoo as possible, this will help to conform to the contours of the skin.

The finished water slide tattoo.

Step 2

To transfer the tattoo, all that is needed is alcohol, a powder puff and the transfer.

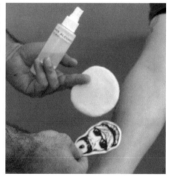

Step 3

Dampen the powder puff with alcohol and then use it to rub a small amount onto the skin. Press the transfer to the skin.

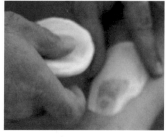

Step 4

Press the puff to the back of the transfer, completely wetting it down. Using too much alcohol will cause the ink on the transfer to run.

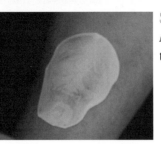

Step 5

Allow the alcohol to dry and then peel off the transfer.

Step 6

The transferred image is shown here. Make-up pencils, alcohol-based make-up or tattoo pens can be used to color this tattoo.

Step 7

Use a tattoo pen, aged ink 75%, to sharpen the lines of the transfer.

Step 8

Aged ink 75% is a black color with a blue tint. Use the pen to fill in and touch up all the line work of the tattoo.

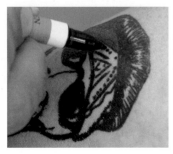

Step 9

A red tattoo pen is used to color the headband in the tattoo. We found the pens very easy to use and very durable.

Step 10

Powder the tattoo with a little pigmented powder.

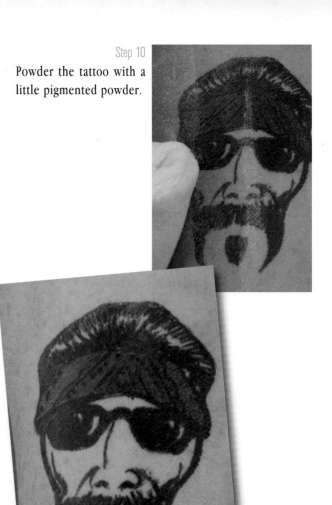

The finished alcohol transfer tattoo

Alternate Transfer Tattoos

Another way of creating a transfer type of tattoo is the same way a real tattoo artist would create a transfer. Using carbon paper over newsprint, draw or copy your design from the carbon paper to the newsprint. Carbon imprint can be transferred from the newsprint to the skin with a little clear deodorant, then the tattoo could be finished, as described above.

MAKE-UP DESIGNORY

Student
Year

Allison Marquez
2006

Student
Year

Evette Smith
2006

Student
Year

Kristy Fuchs
2006

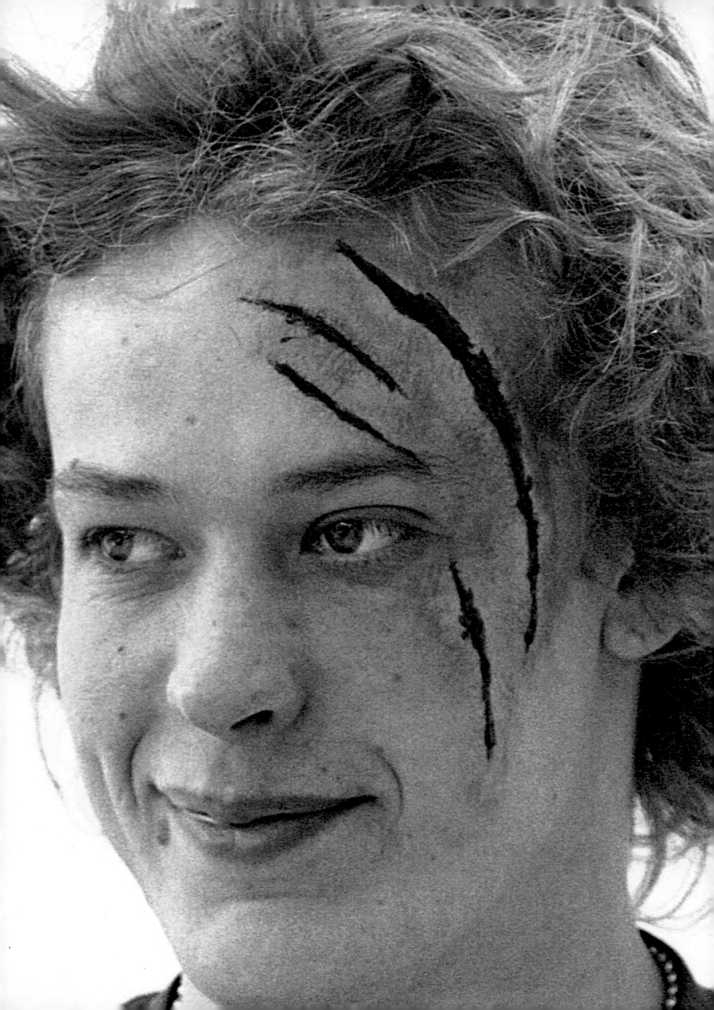

CHAPTER 14

Injury Simulation

This chapter is about injuries and the many different ways they can be accomplished. Often referred to as out-of-the-kit effects, the techniques included will show how to create the same effect different ways. Typically all make-up applications are planned weeks in advance; however oftentimes the make-up artist may not have enough preparation time or the budget to create these effects with prosthetics. Injuries are a common occurrence on productions and the make-up artist should be able to do these simple effects with ease. Since there are several choices of materials to create the same effects, it is up to the make-up artist to become familiar with the material that works best for them. Each of the materials has different properties and may require more supervision than another. Mortician's wax, although an industry standard for years, is very fragile and requires constant touch up. Where as the silicone compound and the prosthetic appliances are more durable. In this chapter we will cover how to do cuts and lacerations, scarring and bullet wounds. The cuts are illustrated using mortician's wax, silicone compound, and generic pre-made prosthetic appliances. The two different types of scarring are created with Rigid Collodion for the indented scar and silicone and Tuplast for the keloid scar. The bullet wound section includes the entrance and the exit wound and how they are created with wax and a prosthetic appliance. This section also includes the use of tubing to create a bleeding effect that can be translated to any of the above-mentioned materials.

Cuts and Lacerations

A cut or laceration is simply a tear to the skin. The depth of the injury will dictate how it is colored and the amount of material needed to create the effect. If the cut is shallow, meaning not very deep, then the inside of the cut should be colored with lighter colors. If it is a deep cut then darker colors are used. Small cuts and lacerations do not need much material to create the look of the wound, however if they are large and there is a need for hanging flesh then more material will be used. Whenever creating a cut reference real photographs, which will help to recreate the injury believably. There are many ways injuries happen and the circumstance will often dictate the look of the wound. Since

an injury is a tear in the skin, create the wound as an opening that tapers to a point on each side. The width of the injury is up to the artist and varies depending on the size of the wound.

Cuts and Lacerations:
Mortician's Wax

The use of wax in make-up goes back to the days long before prosthetics. In almost every special make-up effects project there is a prosthetic appliance used to create a desired effect. So why is it important to learn how to use wax now? Because most projects seen have huge budgets and are well planned. There are however, lots of low budget projects that can't afford prosthetics. There are also situations that arise when a director requires the make-up artist to create something that wasn't originally planned. The artist must be prepared to create whatever effect is needed on a moment's notice. To create a cut made of wax, paint spirit gum or Pros-Aide onto the area where the injury is to be applied. Make sure the area of painted adhesive is not too large and create the shape desired. It is better to paint the adhesive slightly smaller than the desired area. The spirit gum is made tacky by tapping it with a finger. When Pros-Aide dries it leaves a tacky surface. Scoop out a small amount of wax with a palette knife and place between thumb and index finger. Knead the wax until soft, smooth and pliable. Work out any hard spots in the wax.

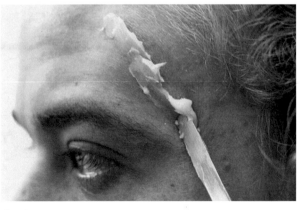

Step 1

Using the palette knife and small pieces of wax build one side of the cut by applying the wax to the skin with gentle pressure.

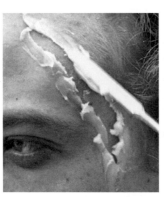

Step 2

Next apply wax to the opposite side of the injury in the same fashion as the first. Keep in mind a straight cut is a boring cut; make it interesting by giving the cut an irregular shape. Each cut will be unique in design and execution.

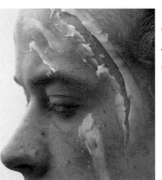

Step 3

This initial application of wax is a rough version of the sculpture.

Step 4

Start on one side of the cut and blend the wax away from the opening of the cut with the palette knife. A light touch is required to get the subtle blend needed.

Step 5

The distance from the top edge of the cut to where it meets the surface of the skin should be, generally, no more than twice the height of the injury.

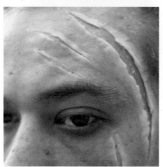

Step 6

The wax is ready to be sealed with latex or plastic sealer. Cut across a white sponge to create a point. The point will minimize the application of the latex.

Step 7

Using the cut wedge sponge stipple a small amount of latex over the entire wax injury. Feather a small amount of latex onto the skin. Dry the latex thoroughly and then powder. Plastic sealer could be used instead of latex on the construction.

Step 8

The method of sealing will dictate which type of make-up is used; for latex use rubber mask grease paint and for plastic sealer use regular make-up. Create a base match and then apply the color very lightly, careful not to over paint a wax construction of this type. Wax is translucent;

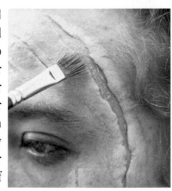

so only apply enough make-up to get the wax to match the surrounding skin. Apply a soft red color to place the natural redness of the skin into the wax. Powder the make-up very carefully, making sure not to damage the construction.

Step 9

Add the bruising that is usually found with this type of injury. Stipple a dark red color over the wax with a brush. This simulates the initial bruising that happens when the skin is damaged.

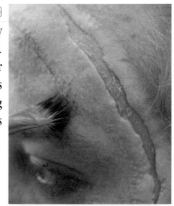

Step 10

Add shadows to the bruise with darker red and purple colors. Maroon may be used wherever needed to create soreness.

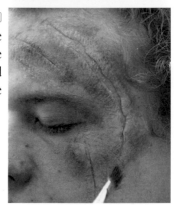

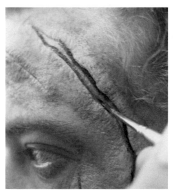

Step 11

Add black inside the cut to create depth or paint black on the inside edge to create a superficial cut.

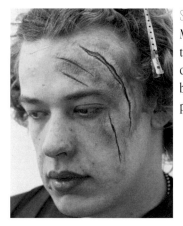

Step 12

Mix up a small amount of thick and runny blood to create blood that looks fresh but will also stay where it is placed.

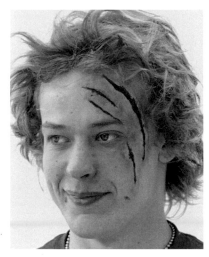

Step 13

More blood can be added on set once the actor is in position and the crew is ready to shoot the effect.

Cuts and Lacerations:
3rd Degree Silicone Modeling Compound

3rd Degree Silicone Modeling Compound is a silicone rubber product that allows an artist to create a variety of injury effects without the use of prosthetics. Construction make-up products, like mortician's wax and 3rd Degree, are beneficial as they allow the artist to design and create the illusion of an injury effect immediately. These products also allow the artist to sculpt and manipulate the shape of the injury directly on the performer's skin. Issues however, may arise in an artists attempt to replicate the effect on a regular basis. Although for quick and single use applications, the cost of creating and applying prosthetic injuries may be unwarranted.

This two-part silicone compound chemically catalyzes, referred to as curing; turning from a workable gel into a flexible solid. The product generally has a predictable cure time of about 5-7 minutes, however may be affected by temperature and humidity. Warm and dry conditions may accelerate the cure time of silicone compounds, while cool and damp conditions will slow the cure time. It is advisable to perform a small batch test based upon the expected working conditions and pace the application of the product accordingly.

Silicone compounds will adhere by nature to the surface of the skin. In areas of excessive movement the artist may ensure adequate adhesion by brushing a preliminary layer of silicone-based adhesive as a primer before applying the silicone compound. Do not use the silicone-modeling compound in a natural hairline as it may become tangled into the hair, which will make it difficult to remove. Areas of the body that may have short or fine body hair may require the artist to apply a primer of adhesive intent upon flattening the body hair to the surface of the skin.

As the product is dispensed onto a make-up palette, the artist can tint the silicone compound using most cream make-up products. The components must be mixed thoroughly on the make-up palette using a palette knife before application. An improper mix of the components may affect the potential cure time of the product, or might result in the product not curing at all. As the product cures, tools or sponges dampened with alcohol may assist the artist with shaping or texturing the silicone compound. 3rd Degree Silicone Modeling Compound may be inhibited by latex and sulfides. The silicone compound should reach full cure before any latex make-up sponges are used.

After the silicone compound has cured, and has been modeled into the desired shape, the product must be sealed with a plastic fixative like Kryolan's Fixer Spray. A plastic fixer spray will allow an artist to adhere color to the surface of the silicone compound. Once sealed with a plastic fixative, an artist has liberty to use many different make-up products. Rubber mask grease paints, cream cosmetics and alcohol-based products, applied in translucent washes and stains are most commonly used.

Remove the injury created in the silicone compound with prosthetic adhesive remover if a primer was applied to the skin. After it has been thoroughly cleaned and rinsed, the artist can utilize the silicone compound "appliance" as continuity reference for future possible applications.

Step 1
Prepare a small amount of cream base, matching the light undertones of the performer's skin tone. Using the 3rd Degree Modeling Silicone compound, mix the two

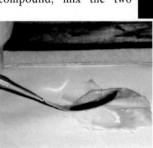

components together on a palette thoroughly. Incorporate a small amount of the performer's cream base into the compound. An accurate base match can tint the silicone compound and intrinsically color the replicated skin tissue.

Step 2
Apply an amount of tinted silicone compound in the shape of cut or injured tissue. Use a palette knife to place and create the general shape of the wound.

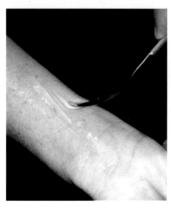

Step 3

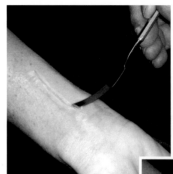

The edge of the cut or wound should blend and taper towards the skin. Use a palette knife sprayed with 99% alcohol to shape and define the opening and interior of the wound.

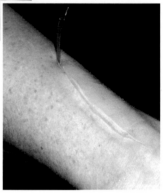

Step 4

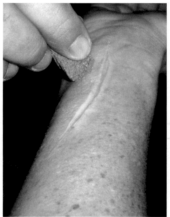

Just before the silicone compound cures, the artist must texture the surface of the open wound. Use the urethane or orange stipple sponge that has been dampened with 99% alcohol. Alcohol prevents the sponge from adhering to the silicone and deposits subtle texture.

Step 5

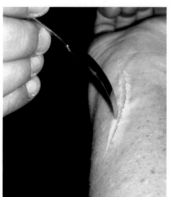

The orange sponge will often press or flatten the opening of a small injury. A small tool, or palette knife sprayed with 99% alcohol can be used to lift and tatter the edge of the ruptured skin and redefine the open wound.

Step 6

At this point, the silicone compound should now be left to cure. Using an orange stipple sponge, apply a generous amount of plastic fixer spray. Continuing to stipple with the sponge as the fixer

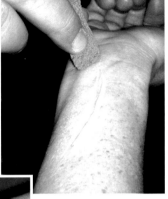

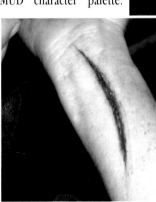

spray dissipates will dry the surface to a matte or satin finish.

Step 7

Create the redness at the opening of the wound using the red from the MUD character palette.

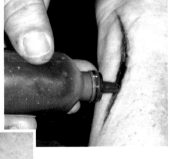

Colors such as maroon, deep purple, and black can add texture and depth to create the look of a freshly opened wound. Powder all cream colors lightly.

Step 8

A small amount of liquid hand soap can be brushed onto the silicone area prior to blood, to prevent the blood from beading up undesirably. Add blood as

needed, use a small brush to direct the flow.

Cuts and Lacerations:
Gelatin Prosthetic Appliance

Gelatin prosthetic appliances have grown in popularity in recent years, and now with foam gelatin pieces being made, it seems gelatin will be around for a while. Both types of pieces are applied in exactly the same way.

This is a station set-up for a gelatin prosthetic make-up. The prosthetic should be sealed prior to application. The excess gelatin around a prosthetic is called flashing and should be kept attached to the prosthetic until the piece is adhered to the skin. To prevent the flashing from accidentally tearing away from the piece, trim away all but an eighth of an inch.

Step 1

Turn the prosthetic face down and gently brush the front and back of the appliance to clean away any mold release with 99% alcohol. This will allow the pros-

thetic to adhere better. Apply Pros-Aide to the back of the piece avoiding the edge and the flashing. Allow the adhesive to dry completely and apply a plastic sealer over it. Repeat this step one additional time.

Step 2

Apply Pros-Aide to the skin in the area the prosthetic will be applied. Allow the adhesive to dry completely. Pros-Aide is clear when dry.

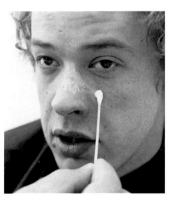

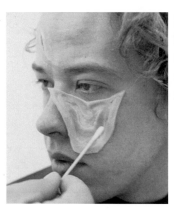

Step 3

Press the prosthetic onto the adhesive, however the edges should not be glued down yet.

Step 4

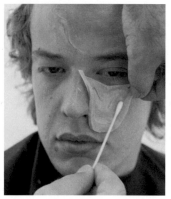

Lift the edge by the flashing and apply the adhesive under it, working all the way around the piece. Firmly press the edge onto the dried adhesive. Be careful not to glue the flashing down.

Step 5

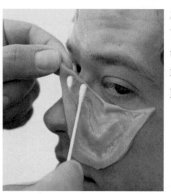

Using a cotton swab, dissolve the edge between the prosthetic and the flashing with witch hazel. Warm water will work, but will cause the edges to become brittle.

Step 6

Use a rolling motion with the cotton swab; push the flashing away from the prosthetic.

Step 7

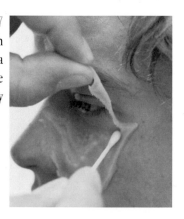

Do not use too much witch hazel because a little goes a long way. 99% alcohol can be used to straighten out any folded edges.

Step 8

Once the flashing is removed and the edge feathered into the skin, use 99% alcohol to straighten and lift any folded edges. Apply Pros-Aide over the edge with the cotton swab to further blend the prosthetic into the skin.

Step 9

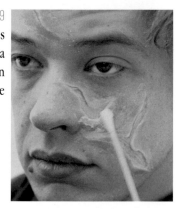

After the prosthetic appliances are completely blended, use a rolling motion to apply a thin coat of Pros-Aide over the entire prosthetic to seal it.

Step 10

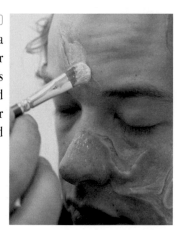

With a filbert brush, pick up a generous amount of powder and press it into the edge. This will help subtle edges blend away. At this point edge filler can be used to further blend any edges.

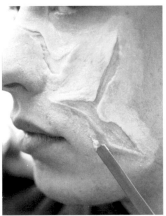

Step 11

Texture can be added to the edge filler two ways; rolling a cotton swab over the wet edge filler or rolling another layer of Pros-Aide over the dried material.

Step 15

Other colors, such as red, green, and yellow, need to be stippled into the appliances to help create a realistic look.

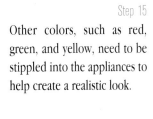

Step 12

Use a cotton swab to apply a plastic sealer over the entire prosthetic. This will further protect the gelatin from moisture and allow the use of regular make-up over the prosthetic.

Step 16

Apply powder over the base colors to set them and to prevent them from mixing with the bruising colors.

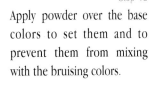

Step 17

Apply the red color over the openings of the cuts and then work the color into the surrounding skin.

Step 13

The gelatin, which is intrinsically colored, will begin to blend into the performer's skin. The gelatin is very translucent so the make-up application should also be. Alcohol based make-ups are excellent to create a realistic texture and color to the prosthetic. The flocking added to the gelatin gives a good base to start from, but additional color should be applied to the piece to create the subtle nuances in the skin.

Step 18

Add maroon as a shadow in various areas. Purple can also be used to make certain areas look sore.

Step 14

Mix the base color with a small amount of 99% alcohol and lightly stipple it over the appliances. Use three or four colors to create a realistic skin texture.

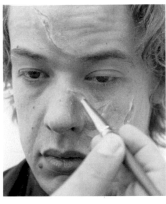
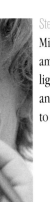

Step 19

Line the opening of the cuts with black. If the inside of the cut is completely painted with a dark color it will look really deep. On the other hand, if make-up is applied along the cdgc of thc inside of the cut it will look more superficial.

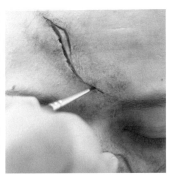

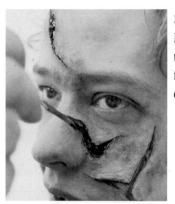

Step 20

Mix regular blood with thick blood to create a fresh meaty look inside each of the cuts.

Step 21

Use the regular blood over the thick blood to get it to run slightly.

Here is the finished make-up. Once on set more blood can be added. Blood is not usually applied to the character until production is ready to shoot it.

Scars

Scars are the result of the skin healing from scrapes, severe burns, cuts, lacerations, surgical wounds and other assorted injuries that may cause damage to the skin. The size and shape of scars follow many of the same principals as those injuries.

For example, unless specifically intended, never make a scar straight because that would look boring. The nature of wounds will cause scarring in a wide variety of shapes and sizes. There are two types of scarring that can be created, indented and raised. Both of these are done almost exactly the same way with the main material being different in each one. For the indented scar we can use Rigid Collodion and for the raised scar we can use Tuplast or 3rd Degree Silicone Modeling Compound.

Indented Scarring:
Rigid Collodion

The first is the indented scar. Apply Pros-Aide to the skin in the desired shape of the scar. Make the adhesive area a little larger than you want the actual scar to be. Do not create an edge with the Pros-Aide. Allow the adhesive to dry completely and then apply Rigid Collodion in the shape of the scar directly over the Pros-Aide. As the Rigid Collodion dries it will begin to shrink, causing the skin to pucker. Pros-Aide is now painted over the entire construction to seal it. Powder the construction to remove the tackiness from the adhesive. Use a small amount of K-Y Jelly to remove any powder residue that may remain on the surface of the adhesive. Next, apply color for the desired effect. The color choice may be red, maroon, brown, purple, or a light flesh color of rubber mask grease paint. Before using Rigid Collodion on any performer do a spot test to ensure there is no adverse reaction to the material.

Step 1

Apply Pros-aide to the skin in the desired shape of the scar. Make the adhesive area a little larger than the actual. Do not create an edge with the Pros-aide.

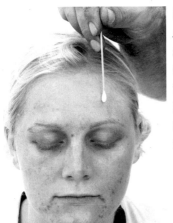

Step 2

Allow the adhesive to dry and then apply Rigid Collodion in the shape of the scar directly over the Pros-aide. As the Rigid Collodion dries it will begin to shrink.

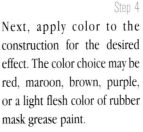

Step 4

Next, apply color to the construction for the desired effect. The color choice may be red, maroon, brown, purple, or a light flesh color of rubber mask grease paint.

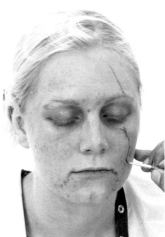

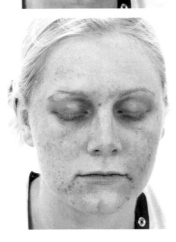

Step 3

Paint Pros-aide over the entire construction to seal it, followed by powder to remove the tackiness of the adhesive. A small amount of K-Y Jelly is used to remove any powder residue that may remain.

The completed scar on our model. Before using Rigid Collodion on any performer do a spot test to ensure there is no adverse reaction to the material.

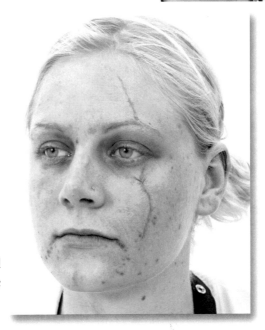

The second is the raised scar or a keloid scar. This type of application can be very similar to the indented scar. Constructing a keloid scar directly on the surface of the skin provides us with two options, 3rd Degree Silicone Modeling compound or Kryolan's Tuplast.

Keloid Scarring:
3rd Degree Silicone Modeling Compound

3rd Degree Silicone Modeling Compound is a silicone rubber product that allows an artist to create a variety of injury effects without the use of prosthetics. This two-part silicone compound chemically catalyzes, also referred to as curing, turning a workable gel into a flexible solid. Silicone compounds will adhere by nature to the surface of the skin; however in areas of excessive movement apply a primer layer of silicone-based adhesive.

As the product is dispensed onto a make-up palette, the artist can tint the silicone compound using most cream make-up products. As the product cures, tools or sponges dampened with alcohol may assist the artist with shaping or texturing the silicone compound.

The silicone compound must be sealed with a plastic fixative. Once sealed with a plastic fixative, silicone compounds can be colored with any make-up product. Translucent washes of rubber mask grease paints, cream cosmetics and alcohol-based products are the most common choices for coloring a silicone compound.

Step 1

Prepare a small amount of cream base, matching the light undertones of the performer's skin tone. Using the 3rd Degree Modeling Silicone compound, mix the two components together on a palette thoroughly. Incorporate a small amount of the performer's cream base into the compound. An accurate base match can tint the silicone compound and intrinsically color the proposed scar tissue.

Step 2

Apply an amount of tinted silicone compound in the shape of the scar. Use a palette knife to place and create the general shape of the scar. Use a palette knife sprayed with 99% alcohol to shape and define the scarred tissue.

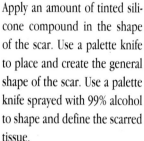
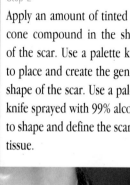

Step 3

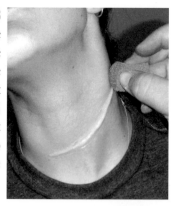

Texture the perimeter of the scarred area just before the silicone compound cures. Use an orange stipple sponge that has been dampened with 99% alcohol. Alcohol will prevent the sponge from adhering to the silicone and deposit subtle texture.

Step 4

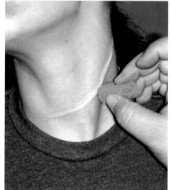

At this point the silicone compound should now be let to cure. Using an orange stipple sponge apply a generous amount of plastic fixer spray. Continuing to stipple with the sponge as the fixer spray dissipates will dry the surface to a matte or satin finish.

Step 5

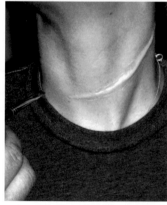

Create the discoloration that often occurs with scarring at the perimeter of the scar. Adding colors such as a soft pink, purples, light flesh or browns from the MUD character palette can create realism and add detail to the look of a scar. Powder all cream colors lightly. K-Y Jelly or an anti-shine can be used to remove excess powder and adjust the shine to the desired level.

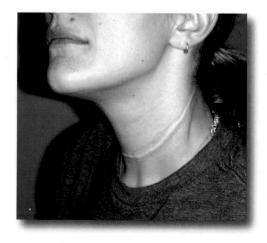

Keloid Scarring:
Tuplast

Kryolan's Tuplast is a thick liquid-plastic material used to create a variety of injury effects including keloid scarring. When using Tuplast, first apply Pros-Aide to the skin in the desired shape of the scar. Make the adhesive area a little larger than the actual scar. Allow the adhesive to dry completely and then apply the scar material in the shape of the scar directly over the Pros-Aide. Immediately brush the scar material with acetone or 99% alcohol to blend the edges and to give the surface some textural lines. Pros-Aide is now painted over the entire construction to seal it. Powder the construction to remove the tackiness from the adhesive and apply a small amount of K-Y Jelly to remove any powder residue that may remain on the surface of the adhesive.

Next, apply color to the construction for the desired effect. An example of a keloid scar created with Tuplast and colored with cream make-up.

Bullet Wounds:
Entrance & Exit

Again, we are using wax to create the effect of a bullet entrance and exit wound and, once again, we would use a prosthetic to do this; what is important about this exercise however, is to use large amounts of wax and make it blend in. Up until now we have used as little product as possible to create the effect, but now, through the use of bullet wounds, you will learn how to deal with large amounts of wax.

Before making our bullet wounds we need to understand what happens when someone is shot. Those that are not familiar with a bullet, still may be aware of the fact that the only part of the bullet that leaves the gun is the very tip. This tip moves at an extremely high rate of speed, about 900 feet to 1200 feet per second. When a bullet hits someone, it appears that the bullet explodes inside of him or her, but that is not the case. What happens is, the bullet enters the body then strikes a bone which is broken from the impact, then the bullet and the bone continue on through the body until they hit something else. This continues until the bullet, and whatever pieces of the person have been ripped out, come shooting out the back. The bullet goes in creating a small hole, but leaving a huge hole as it exits.

The Entrance Wound

To create an entrance wound made of wax, you would apply spirit gum and cotton onto the area where the injury is to be applied, in the same way you would for the cut. Remember, all that should remain are a few fibers of cotton stuck in the spirit gum for the wax to adhere to.

Again, scoop out a small amount of wax with a palette knife placing between your thumb and index finger. Knead the wax until soft, smooth, and pliable, working out any hard spots you may find in it.

The entrance wound is done in the same fashion as the cut. Use the palette knife to apply the wax in a circular shape, leaving the inside edge of the hole sharp and jagged. Blend the outside edge into the skin. This initial application of the wax is considered roughing-out the sculpture only. Blend the wax downward toward the skin with the palette knife. A light touch is required to give you that subtle blend needed. The distance from the top edge of the opening to where it meets the surface of the skin should be, generally, no more than twice the height of the injury.

Using the cut wedge sponge, stipple a small amount of latex over the bullet wound. Dry the latex and then powder it. Also, instead of using latex on the construction you could use plastic sealer.

The method of sealing you chose will dictate which type of make-up you can use. If you chose latex, the make-up you will apply is rubber mask grease paint (RMGP). If you chose plastic sealer, you could use regular make-up over the construction. Because an entrance wound is so small, you should only use just enough make-up to cover the wax. First, create a base match by mixing base colors together until you have achieved the perfect match. Apply the color very lightly; you do not want to over-paint a wax construction of this nature. Next, apply a red color that will replace that natural redness of the skin into the wax, then, powder the make-up very carefully, making sure you do not damage the construction. The next step is to add a subtle amount of bruising color to just the edge. Stipple a dark red color over the edge, where the bullet tore the skin, with a brush. This is to simulate the initial bruising that happens when the skin is damaged. Paint black inside the hole to create depth. Finally, mix up a small amount of thick and runny blood to create a blood that looks fresh but will also stay where you put it; more blood can be added once on set.

The Exit Wound

To create the exit wound, we will be applying larger pieces of wax to the skin on the opposite side of the face, creating a ripped open tear that appears to be missing a few chunks of flesh. With the exit wound we are going to use quite a bit of wax to achieve this effect. You want this injury to look deep and very large. We will also add 1/8 inch tubing into our wound to simulate flowing blood.

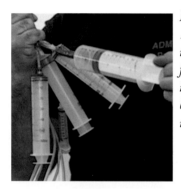

Large syringes attached to 1/8 inch tubing will be used to propel the blood from the wound. The tubing is made of a soft vinyl, but latex tubing can be used as well.

Step 1

The tubes are glued to the face with Pros-aide adhesive. Apply the glue to both the skin and the tubing, allowing each to completely dry, then press the two together. Placement of the tubes is completely up to you and how you want your wound to bleed.

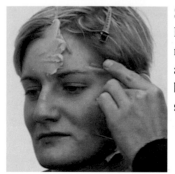

Step 2

Because we are using so much wax you will again use an adhesive and cotton as a base to hold the whole construction in place.

Step 3

The wax will, of course, blend into the skin, but extra care must be taken to smooth the wax as much as possible with the palette knife. As a final step, you may use a small amount of castor oil or hair gel to help smooth out the wax. Be very careful not to use too much or the oil may cause more problems than it solves.

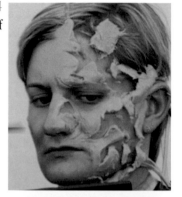

Step 4

The finished application of wax is shown here.

Step 5

Using the cut wedge sponge, stipple several layers of latex over the entire wax injury. Feather a small amount of latex onto the skin. Dry the latex thoroughly, then powder.

Step 6

First, create a base match by mixing rubber mask grease paints together until you have achieved the perfect match. Apply the color all over the wax construction. Wax, by its very nature is quite translucent, but in this case the wax is so thick you have to apply enough base to cover it and then match it to the surrounding skin. You may need to stipple in a few additional base colors to get a good match. Now, apply a red color that will replace that natural redness of the skin into the wax.

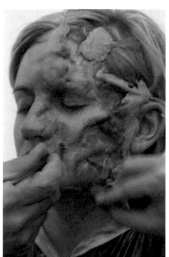

The next step is to add the bruising to our exit wound. First, powder the make-up very carefully, making sure you do not damage the construction. Stipple a dark red color over the wax along the edge with a brush, then stipple more dark red around to color the wax and to create an interesting bruise. To add shadows to the exit wound apply maroon wherever you may need it.

The last thing to do is add our mixture of thick and runny blood to the inside of the injury. This will help to keep the inside of our wound fresh looking. The hair is used to disguise the tubes running to the wound.

Add black inside the various cuts that make up our exit wound to create depth. Put the black only in the deepest areas. The other areas can be painted maroon or a dark red color.

Add thinned blood to each syringe. Hold the syringe above the injury to allow the blood to flow into the tubing. Then lower the syringe to stop the blood from leaking out into the wound.

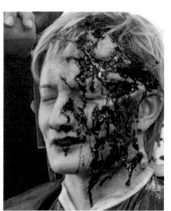

The final effect of the blood oozing from the wound: by squeezing all four syringes at the same time, the blood appears to be flowing from all over inside the wound.

Prosthetic Injury

Prosthetics are the best choice for most injuries because every piece looks the same. As a matter of fact, they are made from the same mold and are exactly the same each day they have to be applied. It is essential in most situations that your make-up matches exactly from day to day. For the following prosthetic make-up we are using a foam gelatin prosthetic. However, an injury prosthetic could be made out of any of the other prosthetic materials referred to in prior chapters.

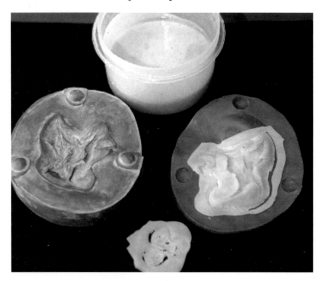

Above is the foam gelatin prosthetic right after it has been de molded. We are using an appliance to simulate a gunshot wound through the cheek. The lower appliances are the entrance wound and the appliance on the mold is the exit wound. Before we start, all of the mold release needs to be removed or washed off the gelatin appliances. Using 99% alcohol and a brush, gently scrub the prosthetic appliances clean. The mold release can cause your prosthetic appliances to not stick to the skin very well.

Step 1

The back of the prosthetic appliance needs to be sealed before it is applied. We use a combination of Pros-aide adhesive and fixer spray. Apply three layers of each, alternating each layer. The Pros-aide is applied first and then the fixer spray. Apply this combination three times.

Step 2

Once the prosthetic has been thoroughly sealed it can be applied to the skin. To attach to the skin apply Pros-aide adhesive to the skin and to the back of the prosthetic. Put two matching spots on the skin and the prosthetic, allowing both to dry, then press them together. Leave about a quarter of an inch of flashing on the prosthetic; this will help keep the edges straight.

Step 3

Apply adhesive to the skin under the appliance, work out to the edges and allow to dry, then press the appliance into the glue. Work all around the prosthetic in this fashion until the edges are secure. Next, use a small amount of witch hazel to dissolve and separate the flashing from the rest of the prosthetic. Be very careful with the witch hazel as a little goes a long way.

Step 4

With the prosthetic completely applied, use Pros-aide and fixer spray over the entire appliance to seal it. This is done in the same way as the inside was sealed. Pros-aide is applied first and allowed to dry, then the fixer spray is applied over the adhesive. All of the Pros-aide must be covered with fixer spray before moving on to color.

Step 5

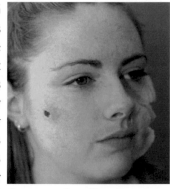

The entrance wound in this make-up was done exactly the same as the larger exit wound. Once both appliances are applied and properly blended, you are now ready to color. Since the prosthetics are so translucent, thin washes of make-up are applied over them helping them blend with the surrounding skin color.

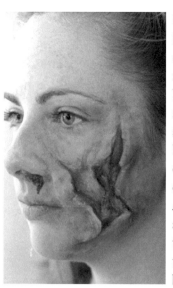

Shadows and highlights can be applied with the same type of make-up as the base color. The bruising colors should also be applied at this point. Make sure you powder between the base colors; and the red bruising colors, ensure that the bruising colors do not become pink. Apply the reds and maroons along the opening of the cut, then apply the bruising into the shadows to help further blend the prosthetic.

Thick and regular blood are mixed together to create a gel blood that has chunks in it. It also helps the blood to stick inside the wound. You can add blood running from the wound once you are on set and the performer is placed.

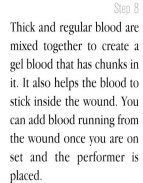

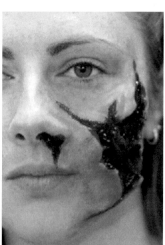

Line the opening of the wound with black and add a little visual interest inside the wound. Red can be painted on the inside to simulate the muscle color and white can be used for the fat and bone.

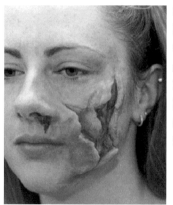

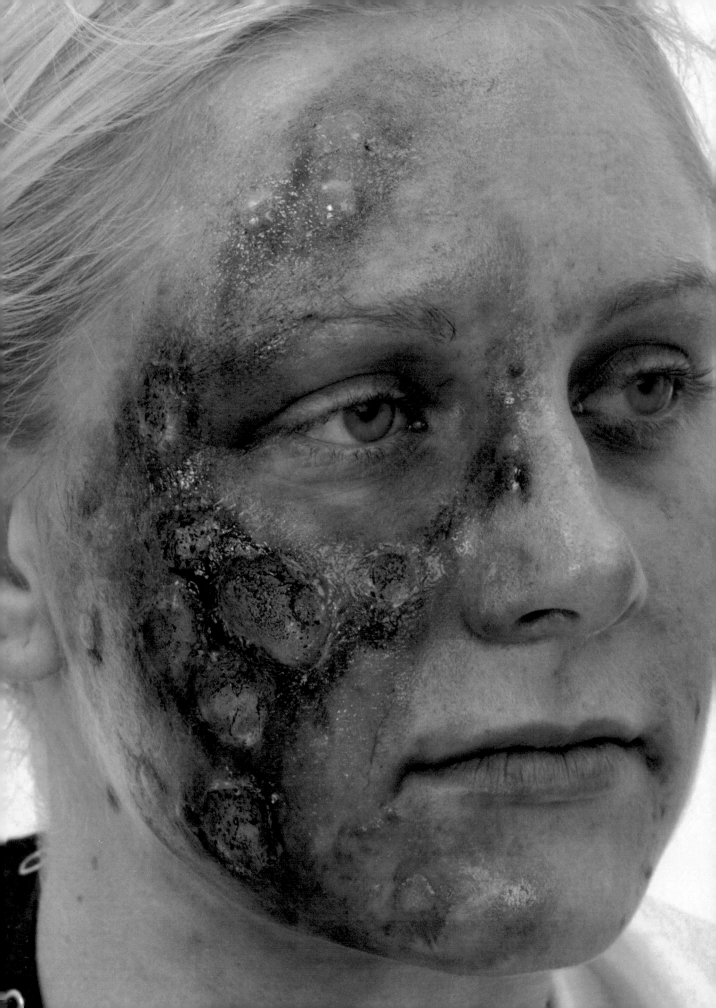

CHAPTER 15

Burns

Many things can cause burns, the most common being fire; but chemicals, water, steam, the sun, and just about anything hot can also cause burns. There are three classifications of burns, first degree, second degree, and third degree. First degree is the least severe while third degree is the worst. The characteristics of a first-degree burn are redness and shine and the most common example is sunburn. A second-degree burn also has the same redness, but is accompanied by blisters. A third-degree burn is the complete and total destruction of skin and is usually surrounded by first and second degree burns; except when caused by something as hot as a branding iron. When creating these burns, it is advisable to have plenty of reference material to view and copy. Proper research is essential in the reproduction of any injury.

First-Degree Burn

Begin with a white sponge and a red color. Cut the edges off the sponge to minimize streaks in the make-up, applying redness with the white sponge in an even pattern. The redder the color, the more severe the burn will appear. When applying to the face for the effect of sunburn, apply the make-up to the high points in the face such as the cheekbones, forehead, and the top of the nose. Apply a layer of K-Y Jelly over the red areas to give them the necessary shine.

Second-Degree Burn

This burn is created somewhat differently, even though it is the same as a first degree with the addition of blisters. First apply Tuplast to the skin in the shape of a bubble, being aware that not all blisters are the same size and shape. Also keep in mind that the placement of each blister should be random and not evenly spaced. Secondly place latex over the blisters with a white sponge. Apply at least three layers making sure to dry each layer with a hair dryer before proceeding to the next. Using a pair of tweezers, tear open the latex that is covering some of the Tuplast. The Tuplast will rip open and the hole will look like a popped blister. Because this construction is made up of latex we must use a RMGP (Rubber Mask Grease

Paint). Choose a bright red color and mix it with a small amount of 99% alcohol; apply it as a wash over the latex construction. Since the latex and Tuplast are translucent, there is no reason to use a flesh color or to heavily cover the construction in make-up. Once a nice red stain is achieved, apply maroon RMGP half way around each blister, alternating the sides of the blister. This will give the illusion of soreness and depth. Lightly apply a small amount of red RMGP into the open blisters. Castor oil mixed with a yellow-green color can be applied to the open blisters to simulate pus.

Third-Degree Burn:
Tuplast And Latex

The third degree burn is the worst of all burns. To properly create this effect, build up layers of skin then tear them off to simulate skin that has been burnt away. Start this burn the same way as the second-degree by applying Tuplast in spots wherever the burn will be most severe. Apply more Tuplast around the area in the shape of blisters. Remember not all blisters are the same size and shape, so make sure they are varied. Also keep in mind that the placement of each blister should be random and not evenly spaced. Latex is applied over the Tuplast to seal it and to create an outer skin for the injury. As soon as the Latex is dry, use tweezers to tear holes into it. The Tuplast used in the severe area should be torn off as well. Again open up some of the blisters too. Just like the second degree burn the construction is made up of latex, which means RMGP must be used. Choose a bright red color and mix it with a small amount of 99% alcohol and apply as a wash over the entire latex construction. The latex and Tuplast are translucent so there is no reason to use a flesh color. Once a nice red stain is achieved over the entire construction simulating the first-degree burn, apply maroon RMGP half way around each blister and on the inside edge of each hole. This will give the illusion of soreness and depth to each blister and to each hole. Lightly apply a small amount of red RMGP into the open blisters. Next, apply black RMGP around each hole and blend out onto the surrounding area. The black simulates charring caused by fire, however if this is a chemical burn there will be no black. As a final touch use a light application of blood inside the holes. Allow the blood to bead up on the surface, creating the look of blood seeping from the burned away areas. Castor oil can be used to give the burn some shine.

Step 1

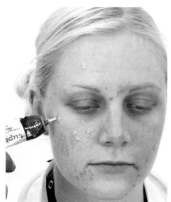

Apply Tuplast to the face in the area that will be most severe and as the blisters that surround the severe area.

Step 2

Next apply latex over all of the Tuplast with a white sponge. Apply at least three layers and make sure you dry each layer with a hair dryer before proceeding to the next.

Step 3

Tear holes in the latex and remove the Tuplast that is in the severe area. The holes in the latex should be of varying sizes and shapes. Tear open the latex that is covering some of the Tuplast in the blister area.

Step 4

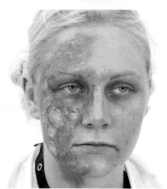

Use a bright red rubber mask grease paint mixed with a small amount of 99% alcohol to color the construction. Apply the color unevenly for a sore look.

Step 5

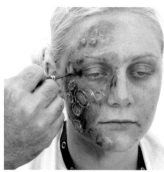

Apply maroon RMGP around each blister and on the inside edge of each opening in the skin. This will give the illusion of soreness and depth to each blister and to each hole.

Step 6

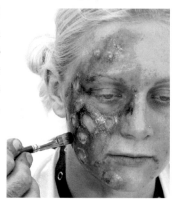

Black is used around each hole and blended out onto the surrounding area. The black make-up simulates the charring caused by fire.

Step 7

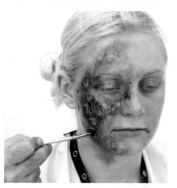

Apply blood to the inside of the holes in the skin. The fake blood will bead up on the surface of the make-up giving the illusion that it is seeping from below.

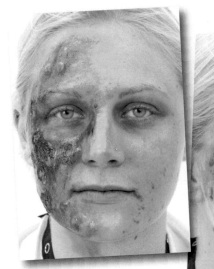

The finished burn

Third-Degree Burn:
3rd Degree Silicone Modeling Compound

The techniques involved in creating this burn use color and shine to simulate the redness and swelling affiliated with the first-degree burn. They also include blistering and use of a deeper maroon color to increase the severity of the burn and achieve the look of a second-degree burn. 3rd Degree Silicone-Modeling Compound will be used to create the illusion of a third degree thermal burn caused by fire or a dry heat source. The full thickness burn area will simulate a broken skin area, exposing the dermis layer and may expose muscle tissue. Fire and smoke will affect the surrounding skin area; black cream and ash powders will be used to simulate this exposure. The resulting burn will demonstrate all aspects of burns and incorporate high contrast of color to achieve soreness and depth, and add a balance of matte and shiny exposure areas. This will replicate glazed and sore areas of the burn, in addition to areas of dry smoke exposure.

The look of a full thickness burn is achieved with several different batches of silicone modeling compound. The first batch of 3rd Degree Silicone modeling compound will be used to create the look of exposed tissue. The silicone-modeling compound is a two-part system. The silicone modeling compound mixes at a 1:1 ratio, equal parts, however if desired the setting time can be accelerated by incorporating a small addition of Part A.

3rd Degree silicone modeling compound may be inhibited by latex and sulfides. The silicone compound should reach full cure before any latex, even latex sponges, are used. A small sample batch should be mixed to accurately assess set or cure time of the silicone material. Temperature and humidity conditions may inhibit or accelerate the curing process. Do not use the silicone-modeling compound in the natural hairline, as it may become tangled into the hair, which will make it difficult to remove.

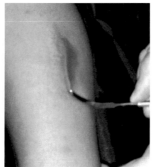

Step 1
Mix the two components together thoroughly, and incorporate

a small amount of red and lake cream color to intrinsically color the tissue layer. Quickly apply a thin layer of silicone compound in the shape of damaged tissue.

Step 2
A palette knife sprayed with 99% alcohol can be used to shape and texture the damaged area. The edge of the silicone construction should blend and taper towards the skin.

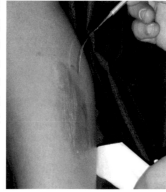

Step 3
Prepare a second batch of silicone modeling compound. The second batch of modeling compound is used to create the illusion of broken skin at the perimeter of the exposed open red area. The silicone-modeling compound

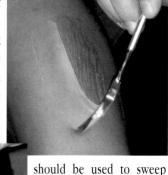

should be used to sweep and transition into the models own skin.

Step 4
As the second batch of silicone cures, use a urethane or orange stipple sponge to texture the surface of the ruptured skin.

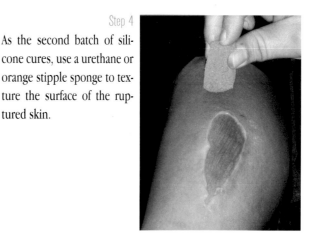

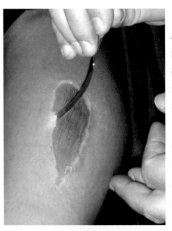

Step 5

A small tool, or palette knife sprayed with 99% alcohol can be used to lift and tatter the edge of the ruptured skin, exposing the damaged tissue. If this step is not completed before the silicone compound cures, a third batch can be used to recreate the look of a ruptured opening.

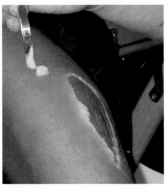

Step 6

Use a third batch, or the remainder of the second batch to create and shape medium and large blisters. Quickly apply the silicone compound in the shape of blisters, using a dabbing motion with a palette knife.

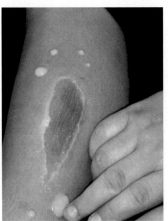

Step 7

Using 99% alcohol on a fingertip, each blister can be rounded and shaped before the silicone cures. It should be stressed that each blister should be unique and vary in size and shape. They should be placed randomly, without regular spacing.

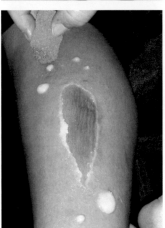

Step 8

After the silicone modeling compound cures, use a white sponge to stipple a generous amount of plastic sealer, such as Kryolan's Fixer Spray over the entire silicone construction burn and each blister area.

Step 9

Latex is stippled with a torn white make-up sponge. The latex is applied unevenly throughout the surface of the burn. The irregular surface of the latex will create texture, simulating the significant damage to the epidermal layer. Using a dry fingertip, roll and distress the broken layers of latex.

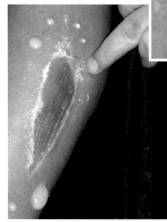

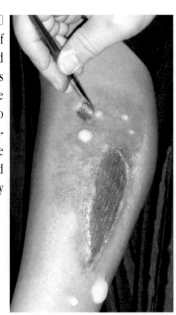

Step 10

Recreate the redness of the burn area using a red color. Apply the redness with a brush or a white make-up sponge; blend to ensure an even application. The severity of the burn can be determined according to the intensity of the cream product.

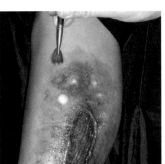

A more severe burn will appear a deeper red and a maroon color is used to stain a drop shadow at the base of each blister. The use of the maroon color will perpetuate the illusion of soreness and depth.

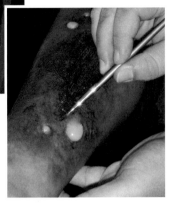

The final touches might include a dusting of black or ash powder. The look of light ash is achieved by mixing a black powder pigment with a small amount of colorless powder. The ash powder can be tapped and smudged as

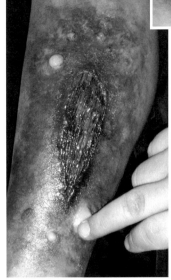

necessary throughout the skin area.

Step 12

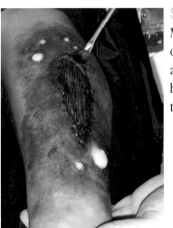

Maroon and black cream color can be mixed with a small amount of 99% alcohol and be applied as a wash throughout the exposed tissue area.

Step 15

KY jelly can be used in the exposed tissue area and the surrounding redness to create shine and swelling. Finally a small amount of blood can be applied at the perimeter of the rupture. A small amount of liquid hand soap can be brushed onto the silicone area prior to blood, to prevent the blood from beading up undesirably.

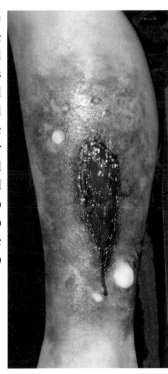

Step 13

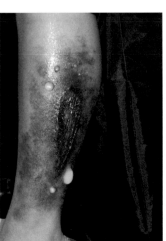

Black cream can be applied around the ruptured opening and blended out into the surrounding area. The black will begin to simulate the charring caused by fire. Powder all cream products lightly.

Third-Degree Burn Variation

This version of a third-degree burn is a more exaggerated version of the first. It is created with gelatin and cotton rather than Tuplast or the silicone compound, but can also be created with gelatin. Apply spirit gum to the skin in the shape of the burn to be created. With a finger, tap the adhesive until it becomes tacky. Press cotton into the adhesive then remove the excess, leaving only small fibers sticking up from the adhesive. Mix a small amount of gelatin with a heated mixture of glycerin and sorbitol. Stir in the gelatin until a creamy consistency is achieved, then add a drop or two of liquid blood for an appropriate color. With a palette knife, spread the gelatin over the edges of the cotton creating a thin edge. Take the remaining gelatin mixture and apply it to the center of the cotton area. Cover all exposed cotton with gelatin. Using a palette knife, manipulate the gelatin and the cotton to look like muscle tissue. Allow the gelatin mixture to dry thoroughly, and apply Tuplast to the skin around it in the shape of blisters. Not all blisters are the same size and shape and they should be varied. Also keep in mind that the placement of each blister should be random and not evenly spaced. Next, apply latex over the blisters and the gelatin with a white sponge. Use at least three layers, making sure you dry each one with a hair dryer before proceeding to the next. Once all the latex is dry, tear holes in the latex, revealing the gelatin beneath. The holes should be of varying sizes and shapes as well. Again, use tweezers to tear open the latex that is covering some of the Tuplast in the blister area. A flesh toned rubber mask grease paint is used to create a realistic skin color and is applied over the skin area of the burn. Next use a bright red color and mix it with a small amount of 99% alcohol, applying it as a wash over the entire latex construction. Once a nice red stain is achieved simulating the first-degree burn, apply maroon RMGP half way around each blister. This time not only will we apply maroon on the inside edge of each hole, but also into each nook and crevice. This will give the illusion of soreness and depth to each blister and hole. Lightly apply a small amount of red RMGP into the open blisters and black RMGP around each hole, blending out onto the surrounding area. The black simulates charring caused by fire and should be very intense around the openings in the skin. Apply a small amount of fake blood inside the holes.

RECENT PROJECTS

MAKE-UP DESIGNORY

STUDENTS

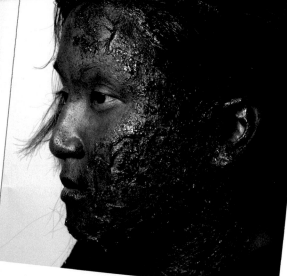

Student
Year

Maija Gundare
2006

Heather Miller
2005

Student
Year

Diana Diaz
2006

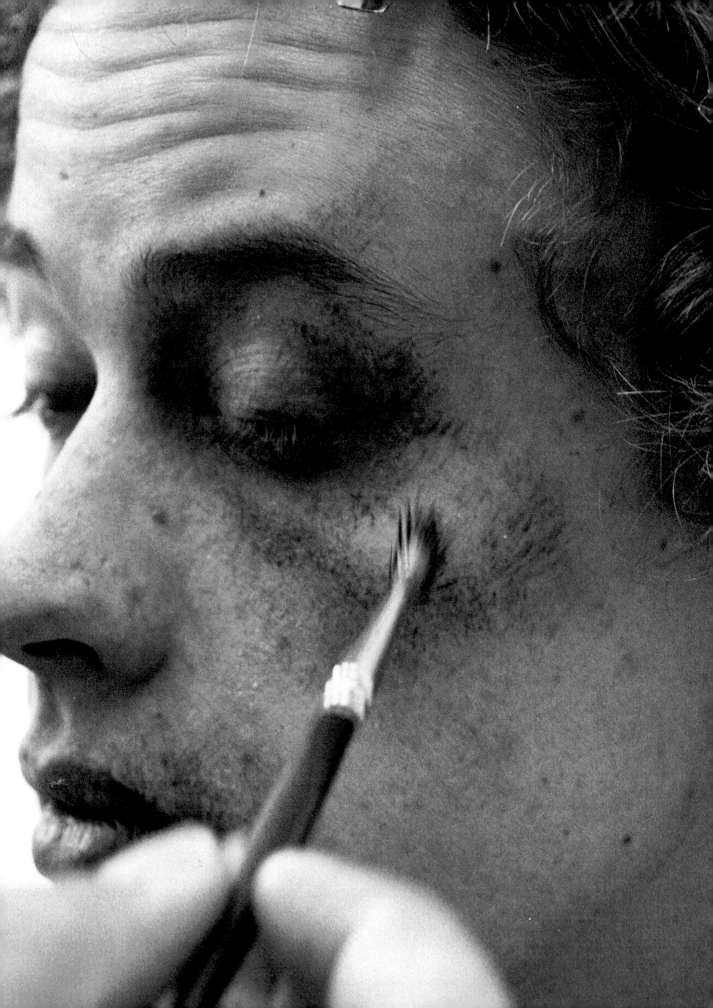

CHAPTER 16

Character Effects

This chapter deals with many simple effects that come up when working as a make-up artist. Usually these can be achieved a variety of ways and we will explore all of the possibilities.

Tears

A typical effect that can happen often in film is crying. Yes, this is an effect. Some actors have the ability to cry on demand, while others may need a moment to think of something really sad. Quite often the make-up artist is required to fill in when actors cannot make themselves cry. The easiest way to accomplish this is by using a menthol blower. The blower is a glass tube with a cap on each end. Place menthol crystals inside the blower between two pieces of cotton and then wrap the end that will be pointed at the actor with a piece of pantyhose. The panty hose will ensure that the crystals will not accidentally be blown into the actor's eye. Then simply aim the end of the tube towards the actor's eye and blow gently. The menthol irritates the eye, causing it to tear. When an actor needs to look like they have been crying for hours, use make-up to redden around the nose and eyes and glycerin to drip down the cheeks. Keep the glycerin out of the actor's eyes.

Sweat

To get the look of perspiration use a mixture of water and glycerin and apply it with a sponge to the areas that need to be shiny. Glycerin will bead up on the skin so if additional beading is necessary use more glycerin than water. Since glycerin is very thick it is easy to maintain continuity. For fight scenes, where the director wants to do a slow motion punch where the actor receiving the punch whips his head around, causing droplets of sweat to fly off of him, use water only. Right before shooting, simply spray the actor down with water and the slow motion camera will pick up every drop.

Dirt

When discussing dirt we need to talk about all kinds of dirt, including, but not limited to grease, oil, mud, dust, grime, ash, soot, etc. First of all, determine what material will be used. Cosmetic manufacturers have a variety of products to help simulate

many of these effects, however sometimes it is best to simply use the real thing. Light and dark powders are great for dirt and dust, whereas eye shadow can be used in some situations. The best solution is to test the ideas prior to the shoot, trying different combinations.

Ice & Snow Effects

Ice and snow are the easy part of this make-up. What we are really creating is a look of severe exposure. Referencing real pictures will give the artist a starting point for the make-up. For this make-up we used more reds to simulate soreness to the skin as well as a pale tone to simulate the lack of blood circulation.

Step 1

Start with a quick 1st degree burn to the face simulating windburn. Begin with a white sponge and a red color. Cut the edges off the white sponge to minimize streaks in the make-up. The redder the color, the more severe the burn will appear. Apply the

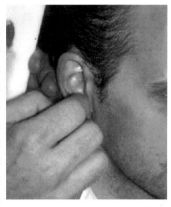

make-up to the high points in the face such as the cheekbones, forehead, and the top of the nose.

Step 2

An orange sponge can also be used to apply the colors to the face. The nice thing about the orange sponge is the texture it will create on the skin. Stipple on both the red and the pale base.

Apply the pale base over the high areas of the face. This will help sink in the eyes a little and give the skin in an unhealthy condition. Add a little blue to the eyelid area and the lips. Ultra Ice will be applied next.

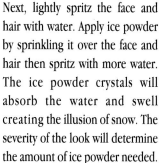

Next, lightly spritz the face and hair with water. Apply ice powder by sprinkling it over the face and hair then spritz with more water. The ice powder crystals will absorb the water and swell creating the illusion of snow. The severity of the look will determine the amount of ice powder needed.

Ultra Ice is a gel material that simulates ice on the skin. Using a pallet knife apply the gel in the hair, to the tip of the nose, eyebrows, and ears. Applying it heavily and allowing it to remain sharp in parts can create icicles.

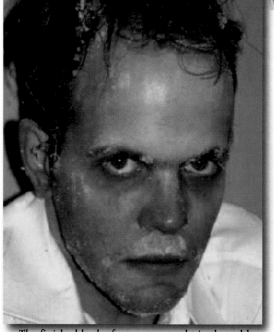

The finished look of someone caught in the cold and left to the elements.

Blood Formula

There are as many blood formulas as there are make-up artists, with most of them creating a believable effect. However, when a film requires a bleeding effect it is usually advisable to purchase fake blood from a manufacturer. There are three reasons to buy blood rather than make your own. First, the color of the blood that most manufacturers are creating is believable and will match even when using different bottles. The thickness and translucency of the blood available is quite good. Secondarily, the cost of buying pre-made blood is about the same as driving around and picking up the ingredients, plus the time involved in mixing it up in the kitchen. When looking at cost factors along with time and effort, it is more cost effective to purchase it pre-made. Finally, and maybe most importantly, if an actor has an adverse reaction to the blood the liability rests solely on the shoulders of the manufacturer. As long as it is used within the guidelines the manufacturer sets.

This is a classic formula used by many artists starting out. It has subsequently been expanded upon and developed to suit individual needs. Start with a quart of Karo syrup and add red food coloring to get a good clear bright red. Add 2 drops of green and one drop of blue to give the blood a dark undertone. Cornstarch is used to give the proper thickness; it is added slowly until the right thickness is achieved.

Blood Knife

We are referring to a gag that makes it appear as if someone is cut with a real knife.

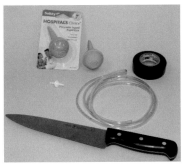

Step 1

Shown are the materials required to create the blood knife effect: ball syringe, an eighth inch inside diameter tubing, tubing connector, black electrical tape, and a real knife.

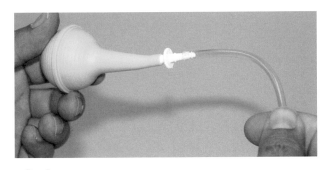

Step 2

Slip the connector into the ball syringe and attach the tubing to the connector. The ball syringe is attached only to help with the placement.

Step 3

The knife is real so dull it before use. A Dremel is used to flatten the edge of the knife; however anything that will grind down metal will work.

Step 4

Using black electrical tape, attach the connector and the ball syringe to the handle. Ensure the tubing will be on the side facing away from camera.

Step 5

Next tape the tubing into position. Run it close to the cutting edge of the blade.

Step 6

Cut the tubing to length. Cut the tube at an angle so the end is a little easier to hide.

Step 7

Use electrical tape to close the end, and then tape it down to the knife. Again make sure the tube is close to the cutting edge of the knife.

Step 8

Cut away the tape holding the ball syringe. Re-tape the connector to ensure it does not move. The ball syringe is removable, allowing for easy filling.

Step 9

A piece of tape is applied along the back of the tubing to ensure it does not move when blood is pumped through it. Use an X-acto knife to cut small slits into the bottom of the tube. The blood will flow from these small slits.

Step 10

Pour blood into a separate container. Add water if the blood is too thick to flow easily through the tubing. Squeeze the ball syringe while inserting the blood; releasing the pressure will fill it.

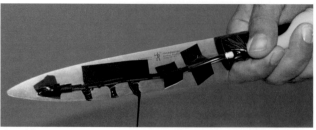

Step 12

Squeezing the syringe causes the blood to ooze out of the slits in the tube.

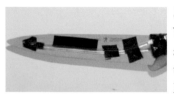

Step 11

Wipe off any excess blood and push the syringe onto the connector. The finished knife is ready to be used.

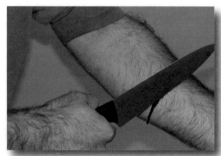  

Prior to doing the effect on camera, instruct the actor on how to use the knife. Place the blade to the skin and drag it across the skin while squeezing the syringe. The knife will create a nice straight line of blood, giving the illusion that the knife is really cutting into the skin. This needs to be a quick type of an effect, if the camera lingers on the cut it will spoil the effect.

Bladders

Bladders are small latex pockets used to create an on-camera swelling effect. They are applied under a prosthetic appliance and inflated with air to make it appear as if the skin is swelling. This can be used for a multitude of effects. The way bladders are made can also be used to create flat tubing, such as for an exit wound. The following is a step-by-step process for a bladder or flat tube.

Step 2

In this demonstration we are using the same size bladder over and over, but the bladder can be a variety of shapes and sizes, with no limit to the possibilities.

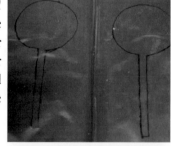

Step 1

First, draw the design for the bladder on a piece of white paper and then cut out the shape, making a template. Trace the template onto a piece of black plastic, such as a black trash bag. This allows multiple pieces of plastic to be cut from one template.

Step 3

Any smooth surface will work to build the bladder. We are using a piece of wood that was waxed and buffed smooth. Lay the cut out pieces of plastic on the board.and draw a line around them about a quarter of an inch away. This will allow for sturdy edges around the bladder.

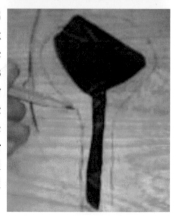

Step 4

Remove the plastic and stipple latex onto the board over the drawn on bladders. Four layers will be needed. Stipple the first layer onto the board, then allow to dry half way. Apply each of the four layers in the same fashion. The layers of latex will bond to each other better if they are only half dry. Be careful not to damage the previous layer with the application of the subsequent layer.

Step 5

Lay the cut pieces of plastic onto the fourth layer and again do not allow the latex to fully dry. Position the plastic carefully onto the latex, centering the piece. Once in place stipple a layer of latex over the plastic and the other layers of latex. Apply the latex in the same fashion as before, with four layers of latex on top of the plastic.

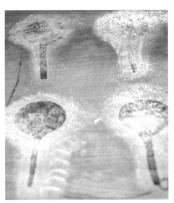

Step 6

Allow the whole thing to dry properly. Removing the bladder too soon may cause a small hole or tear to develop.

Step 7

Powder the entire bladder or the un-powdered latex will stick to itself.

Step 8

Carefully lift the edge of the bladder up and powder the bottom side of the piece. Peel the whole piece off the board. Once the bladder is removed, powder it and trim off the excess edge.

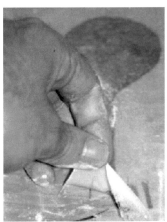

Step 9

Cut the end off the bladder's long tail, exposing the plastic. Fill a ball syringe with powder and force air and powder into the bladder. The powder will coat the interior of the bladder and keep it from sticking to itself. Once there is a sufficient amount of powder inside the bladder, use a pair of tweezers to pull the plastic out. The plastic could be left in place if inflating the bladder with air. However, if fluid is to flow through the bladder then the plastic will need to be removed. The bladder is now ready to be applied under a prosthetic.

Applying Bladders

For a bladder to work properly it must have enough room to expand. Only apply adhesive to the center bottom, the part of the bladder that touches the skin. Also, only apply the prosthetic around the bladder. No glue should be on top of the bladder; the adhesive used for the prosthetic should go around the bladder.

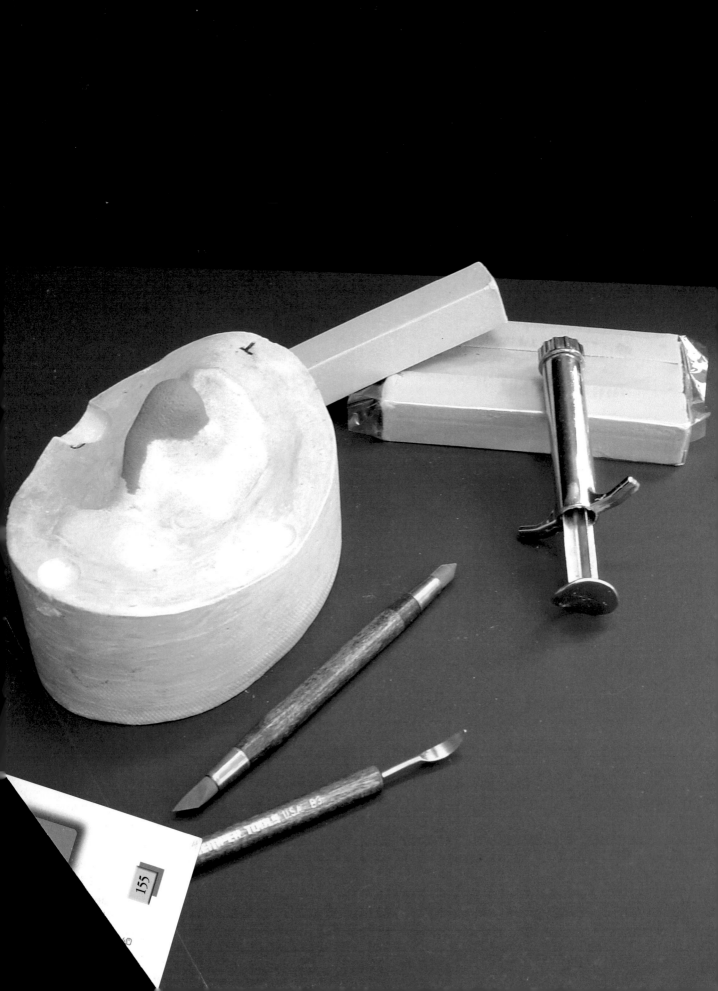

CHAPTER 17

Working as a Make-up Artist

For a make-up artist, understanding how the entertainment business works is as important as knowing how to apply eye shadow. This chapter will cover the aspects of the make-up profession often overlooked. Working as a professional make-up artist is comparable to running a small business. It is a freelance business that requires the artist to be organized and have a well thought out plan. The plan should include a portfolio, resume, business cards and career goals. There are several industries available to a make-up artist and some artist may work in more than one. A film and television make-up artist is a person that works on feature films, independent films, documentaries, television shows, sitcoms, soap operas, award shows, commercials, and infomercials. A fashion make-up artist is a person that works on commercials, advertising, editorial campaigns for magazines, album covers, catalogues, music videos, concerts, fashion shows, and magazine covers. In theater the make-up artist can work on plays, musicals, opera, and live performances. A key element to a successful career is choosing an area of make-up that interests the artist. Research successful artists in the industry of choice and find out what made them successful.

Freelancing

A freelancer is a person that sells his or her services to employers without a long-term commitment. There are two ways a make-up artist can be hired; one is to be hired as an employee and the other is to be hired as a subcontractor. When hired as an employee, the employer withholds taxes and pays into state compensation funds. A subcontractor on the other hand is required to withhold taxes and is responsible to pay any state compensation. As a result the artist will need to charge more on a project that requires them to be a subcontractor. Freelance artists are required to find work, negotiate rates, handle all logistics associated with a job, track and collect all payments, network with decision makers, and keep themselves up to date on all changes and advances in the industry. Establishing a day rate can sometimes be difficult and requires the artist to figure out what they are worth. Some good ways to figure out a day rate is to speak with peers and to research how much a particular industry pays. Discuss every aspect of being paid with decision makers including the terms and conditions of the assignment. Confirm how and when the payment will be made. Once hired it is important to respect the commitments made, always give 110 percent no matter how much is being paid. Remember, nothing is more dishonorable than backing out of a job last minute for a higher paying job or worse not doing the best job possible because it is low paying. Once all the details are agreed to the paperwork mill starts for the freelance artist. Typically the contract is the form used to spell out all the details of the job. This form may be called a 'deal memo' or a 'confirmation,' however it is a contract and should be viewed as such. If hired as an employee then usually this is all that is needed, but if subcontracting the artist needs to submit an invoice at the end of the project in order to be paid.

Assisting

This is a great way to learn without being responsible for the outcome of a project. It also allows the artist to learn set etiquette, politics, tips, and techniques. There is assisting etiquette that must be observed to do well. As an assistant the artist may be asked to do all sorts of odd things like running errands, setting up and packing the lead artist's kit, cleaning brushes and cutting sponges. The opportunity to see and experience a shoot and how another artist works is invaluable in developing as an artist. Stay open to suggestions, be grateful for help received and never get defensive. Assisting is not an opportunity to ask a ton of questions of the lead artist or to exploit this opportunity for personal gain. The assistant is there to support the lead artist and to make them look good.

Portfolio

The requirements of the portfolio vary depending on which area of make-up an artist works. It needs to be as diverse as possible regardless of the industry. Showing a range of different types of make-up is essential to illustrate what an artist can achieve. For the fashion industry, the portfolio should have large beautiful pictures of fashion make-ups with out any visual defects. Typically the pictures are retouched, however we believe there should only be a minimal amount of retouching so that the artist's true work can be viewed. Pictures should show a range from natural to avant-garde make-up. As a film artist the pictures do not need to be large and perfect and usually are not retouched. The portfolio often includes pictures taken by the artist between takes or in the make-up trailer. Again, the portfolio should show a range of abilities. Included in the portfolio should also be natural make-ups as well as make-up effects. In film and television the need for a portfolio diminishes as an artist becomes more successful. Theater has a different set of requirements; the portfolio should not only include pictures of make-up created for the theater, but should also include the designs for the make-ups. Once again, showing a range of work is very important. Decision makers often have a hard time imagining that the artist is capable of a make-up if they do not see it in the portfolio.

Website

The portfolio has been the center of an artist's marketing campaign for years; however the website is very quickly going to replace the portfolio entirely. This is the information age and every artist should have a website that mirrors the portfolio. A website is a page on the Internet that features a particular person or product. The site should include a bio of the artist, contact information, a resume, and a section for pictures. The wonderful thing about having a site is anyone in the world anywhere in the world can instantly access the site and look at the portfolio. Creating a website has become less expensive than in previous years and there are a variety of ways to set one up. Most make-up artists do not know how to build a website and that usually keeps them from making one. The main elements needed are a domain name, web designer, and hosting company. The domain name can be purchased on the Internet and needs to be renewed annually. It can be anything desired, such as "Yourname.com." The website designer creates the actual website with information provided by the artist and will send the completed site to a hosting company. A hosting company manages the site on the Internet; they provide the server where the site will actually be located. There are several companies and individuals that can handle all aspects of a website, but may be more expensive. Realize creating a website can be done on a very low budget. By using a student web designer and searching the Internet for the least expensive hosting company, an artist can have a website built for free and only pay a low monthly charge. One additional benefit to having a real website is a personalized email address that will not change; for example Make-up@Yourname.com. There are also numerous free websites available to artists that can be utilized for absolutely no money.

Resume

In some cases a resume is as important as having a portfolio and should absolutely be on the website. The primary component to a resume is work experience, which explains the artist's responsibilities on different jobs. Also included is relevant information like skills and education. Resumes are different from the film and television to fashion industries. Film resumes list an enormous amount of information, such as a production company, director, producer, artist title, and project name. This type highlights the responsibilities the artist undertook. A resume for the theater looks similar to the film version, while fashion is more concerned with who the artist worked with, such as photographers, magazines, directors, celebrities, and clients. Try to keep the information to one page and make it as professional looking as possible, more than likely it will be sent to prospective employers in email form.

Business Cards

The business card is one of the simplest tools acquired. Putting together a piece that is both effective marketing and esthetically pleasing is the hard part. Without a business card an artist will not have an essential tool for getting work. It is the least expensive way to let someone know who we are, what it is we do, and how to contact us. The card should contain the artist's name, phone number, occupation, and email address. The phone number should be a cell phone that will stay with the artist for years, even if the carrier changes. The voice mail message should be professional and short, friends will understand if there is not a funny or laid back message. There should be only one occupation listed on the card, nothing says undecided like Make-up Artist/Photographer. Keep it simple like Make-up Artist, Hairstylist, or Special Make-up Effects. Finally the email address should be professional, save any cute or pet names for friends. The address on the card should either be connected to the artist's website or to a public address like Gmail. An address connected to an Internet provider may change where a public address usually doesn't.

Attitude

Attitude is the single most important tool possessed by the artist. A good attitude will take the artist places talent will never be able to reach. Filmmaking, and just about every industry that uses a make-up artist, is an art form that is a collaboration of many talents. The truth is production would rather hire a person with a good attitude and personality than the most talented artist. When we say good attitude what do we mean? The first is a positive attitude, always in a good mood and smiling, willing to help in every way possible, and anticipating the actors' and production's needs at all times.

Now, all this niceness may make a few nauseous, but what we are saying is, when working on set always realize the next job can come from anywhere and anyone. So be respectful of every person whether it is the director or an extra.

Continuity

One of the more important aspects of our job is to maintain continuity of the make-up. Film and television projects take a long time to make and some scenes may take several days to film, sometimes only representing a few minutes on screen. Our job is to ensure we are using the same colors on the actors every day, making sure when the scene is cut together there are no changes in the make-up. There are many ways artists maintain continuity, one being with a camera. Some artists still use Polaroid cameras, however most use digital cameras. The process is quite simple; take a picture of the actor following the establishing shot, this way changes made on set will be recorded. Print the picture using a small photo printer and write the scene number on the back. All of the photographs will be labeled with the correct scene number for later reference. Another way to maintain continuity is to write good notes on how each make-up is done; some projects may require both techniques.

Face Charts

A face chart is a tool used by an artist to design make-up and convey those designs to other artists or production. This is in addition to showing how the idea will lay out on the face. A face chart is also a great tool for the theater when the make-up artist needs to teach the actors how to put on their make-up. The chart can show the design and list the steps and colors used to create the look. It can also be used for continuity purposes; by outlining the make-up an artist will know what color to use and where to place it. This is especially helpful when doing pick up shots.

Test Shoot

These shoots are often an under-used tool in a production's bag of tricks. Whenever starting a project that requires a character make-up outside the norm of beauty make-up, request a test shoot. A test shoot is done prior to the first day of actual shooting. The camera is rented and film is purchased. The planned make-up is done and a day later the film is processed, giving the opportunity to view the character on screen and analyze the effect. Current advancements in filming allow the artist to view the make-up the same day it is shot. This alleviates the wait time for processing. Any necessary adjustments based on what is seen can be made once the shoot begins. This also gives production a clear idea of what to expect on the first day of shooting.

Script Breakdown

This is the first step in any production with a story. Even commercials and music videos need a breakdown. It is the responsibility of the make-up artist to first read the script and then takes notes on it. Never be that person on set asking what is going on. You want to know what is happening at all times. The best way to do this is to read the script and understand it completely, we recommend reading it twice. The first time read it in order to understand the story. The second time highlight all of the characters and their different make-ups. The script may read, "Bob enters the room meeting Teri for the first time." Since this is the first time we are meeting Teri in the script, her name or the line on which it appears, should be highlighted. By the same token if the script says "Teri turns and punches Bob in the nose," highlight this line to indicate that a make-up change happens. Once all make-up aspects of the project have been highlighted, write in scene order which actors are in the scene and what their make-up is. If there are questions for production about a character such as, "Do you want Bob's nose to bleed?" write it down on a separate piece of paper with the scene number. Bring this paper to the production meeting and get all questions answered by the appropriate person. The script breakdown is also a start to keeping accurate records and doing a good job with continuity.

Creativity

Often we hear from beginning make-up artists that they are not very creative. It is actually impossible for a relatively normal human being to not be creative. Every time we get lost we must be creative to figure out a solution. Every person has their own way of handling situations which is usually based on some past experience. Creativity is often times the sum of our experiences. This is not a classical definition of creativity, nor do we want to expound upon this concept as it has been done for hundreds of years. We can train ourselves to be creative by simply expanding our experiences and looking for new ways to translate them. For example, when asked to create an alien the artist could simply say it is impossible to create something new or they can look to their experiences. An experience is something seen or an event. So the artist could choose three known animals and start to mix their individual elements until they created something that looked like an alien. If we asked for an alien and specified that we wanted it to have the qualities of an elephant, a grasshopper, and an alligator, each person reading this would start to assemble those three animals in different ways. Most artists could assemble the animals in at least five different looks. When parameters are specified it is actually quite easy to be creative. If for some reason the three animals looked unfamiliar then a simple search of the Internet would expand the artists' experience. Understanding the creative process will help some artists to be more creative. In an effort to beat a dead horse, let us look at one more example; if an artist was asked to do a fashion show with an edgy make-up design, then the artist would simply look at other edgy make-ups, funky designs that apply to different industries, and speak with the clothing designer for the show. By doing this the artist will be able to design a look that is original and in line with what the designer wants.

Research

Research is an essential tool when creating the best look and effect. Whether doing a realistic aging make-up or the current trends in eye shadow, it is nice to start off with a basic idea of what could be done. Research is a term we use to describe the process of looking at reality and then building those elements into our make-up. It does not matter if looking at other artist creations or at real life. Research can be the source of inspiration for a character by incorporating elements we see in the everyday world. The Internet is by far the best research tool on the planet; however there are many other places an artist can do research. Public libraries or school libraries are usually filled with reference material.

Set Etiquette

The subject of etiquette can also be called professionalism. Attitude is everything on a set; respect everyone in the crew because the next job may come from one of them. Working in the entertainment industry is a long process and often there is a lot of sitting around and doing nothing. Knowing how to act and behave on set as well as interviews will greatly help with career goals. The artist's physical appearance including the make-up kit and bag, should be neat and clean at all times. Additionally get enough sleep, stay in good health and maintain good habits. Arrive early for every aspect of the job, there is never a reason for being late. When working in film or fashion industries, stay close to the camera. The artist must be ready to do a touch up on a moments notice. Always try to be proactive, making sure the actors are ready for camera.. Never leave the set; someone from the make-up department must always be present. Actors tend to tell their make-up artists everything, even very personal information. As a professional, it is never okay to disclose this information to anyone. The best piece of advice we could give to a new make-up artist is to be a good listener.

Touch Ups

When learning make-up it is hard to understand what a touch up is until actually doing make-up on a project. It is the responsibility of the make-up artist to make sure the character's make-up, whether it is beauty or an elaborate prosthetic, looks the same as when it was applied. This is the essence of touching up make-up. There should be no reason to rush in between every take to powder the actor. Rather, there should only be a touch up when a problem needs to be corrected; if there is unwanted shine then go in and fix it. The job of a make-up artist is to be close to the camera, keeping an eye on make-up. Doing a touch up is very similar to doing the initial make-up application. The artist should have the same colors, materials, and tools used. Prior to going to set, put together a set bag that contains all of the materials needed to fix just about any problem. A common mistake is to simply powder everyone as a way of touching them up. The actor should only be powdered a few times a day. In most cases a tissue wrapped around a powder puff can be used to absorb excess oil. An excess of powdering the actor will result in a muddy make-up.

The Make-up Kit

The make-up kit is the artist's toolbox. There is a list of tools in Chapter One that gives an idea of the utensils needed to work as a make-up artist; these should be in the kit. In addition to these tools is all the make-up needed to complete a particular project. The following is a list of additional items that might be needed in the kit as well as the make-up trailer. There is no need to carry everything all the time but rather separate items into smaller bags or kits that can be used for specific projects. A professional make-up artist should be prepared for any eventuality. This is not always possible but we do try.

Additional Items for your Kit

Cell Phone	Business Cards
Application Notes	Utility Bag
Rubber Bands	Pencil Sharpener
Sewing Kit	Shaving Cream
Zip Lock Bags	Washcloths
Ever Blum (cosmetic stain remover)	35mm or Digital Camera
Moisturizer	Super Matte Anti-shine
Make-up Remover Towelettes	Small On-set Chair
Swiss Army Knife or Small Tool Kit	Eye Dropper
Mints	Gum
Toothbrush	Toothpaste
Mouthwash	Hand Held Mirror
Straws	Make-up Chair
Breath Spray	Oil Absorbing Spray
Non-latex Make-up Sponge	Sharpie Marker

Mascara	Concealers
Empty Container for Brush Cleaner	Small Plastic Cups
Eye Lash Curler	Double Sided Tape
Scotch Tape	Safety Pins
Visine	Super Glue
Emery Board	Cotton Balls
Nail Polish Remover	Nail Clippers
Glycerin (sweat)	Extra Spray Bottles
Sea Sponge	Blood Capsules
Small container to stand up pencils and brushes	

Hair Supplies

Headbands	Bobby Pins
Hairpins	Hair Spray
Spray Shine	Thermal Set Mist
Curl Relax Balm	Styling Glaze
Spray Gel	Mousse
Hot Rollers	Roller Clamps
Clips	Wave Clamps
Marcelle Grip Curling Irons	Hair Dryer
Hair Ribbons	Hair Bands
Coated Ponytail Holders	Squeeze Type Hair Clips
Extension Cord	Plug Adapter
Tint Brush	Hair White
Wig Cap	Electric Clippers
Brushes - Round, Vented, Thermal and Styling	
Combs - Wide Tooth, Rat Tail, Styling Hair Pick	

Personal Items For Location Shooting

Hip Pack	Water
Vitamins	Personal Bag (Back Pack)
Pillow	Bathroom Supplies

Desert / Hot Location

Sunscreen	Hat
Small Cooler for on Set Make-up	Sunglasses
Bandana (to wet around neck)	Umbrella
Mister or Spray Bottle with Fan	Aloe Vera Gel

Make-up Artist's First Aid Kit

Generic First Aid Kit	Bar of Soap
Feminine Hygiene Products	Aspirin & Tylenol
Dental Floss	Throat Lozenges
Cold Remedies	

Media

We could write a complete book for every medium and how each make-up relates to it. Instead, we thought we would shed some light on these subjects individually. Some artists work in one area, whereas other artists may work in multiple areas. When asked how to paint a prosthetic appliance, the question "in which medium?" should always arise. Depending on the way we are viewing that prosthetic appliance, it may require different ways of coloring. The way we shoot things has changed so drastically over the past few years; there is no standard answer for any make-up technique.

There is a lot of talk about how critical a medium may be. High definition has drawn attention to the fact that make-up has to be more subtle than in previous formats. In addition to that fact there has been a tremendous amount of misinformation about Hi-Def. We have heard artists say in the past that with Hi-Def the audience can see brush strokes in the make-up. They have also stated that the make-up needs to be applied with an airbrush to look right. Both statements would be incorrect. The reality is, that the process of recording an image has improved drastically, however Hi-Def although very clear and detailed, is similar to film. Actually it has gotten so close, that studios are starting to shoot feature films with Hi-Def cameras. Many artists that typically work in television are shocked by the clarity of Hi-Def. A high definition image is far superior to an analog video image, so an artist could easily believe it has the best quality. What is actually happening is that the techniques employed for film are now being applied to television; the subtle type of make-up is becoming the norm. This means that artists working in film and television are doing the same types of make-up. Soon high definition will be the choice for production companies because they can also see footage immediately without processing. Beyond film and television, photographers are almost exclusively shooting digitally. The main reason is the ease of use; the photographer can deliver a project faster.

Film

Film when viewed, is a very large image and can be one of the most critical. What this means for make-up artist is that the make-up needs to look very natural. For large budget projects 70-millimeter film is usually selected. Cinematographers still prefer film to high definition because of the depth shown. With film, each frame is exposed to light that bounces off the subject and burns different colors onto the negative filmstrip. The colors we choose will stay true. With film production it is "what you see is what you get." That means a very natural make-up should be applied rather than a heavy or obvious application. Where the film is viewed will also affect the decisions on which make-up techniques should be used. Working on a feature film that will be shown in a theater requires the make-up to be thin and natural. If filming a television show then there are more options in terms of the types of make-ups done.

Television

Television refers to the way projects are viewed, not how they are shot. With the advent of high definition, television has become more like film. Most studios have switched over to high definition and with the exception of some smaller markets an artist would be hard pressed to find a television station broadcasting an analog signal. The airbrush has become very popular to use on television shows, however this is mainly due to the misinformation described earlier regarding high definition and image quality. The airbrush is a great tool for applying make-up, but keep in mind it is just another tool in an artist's arsenal.

Print

Print is probably the most critical of all media simply because it is a non-moving frame of film. Print includes both digital prints and film prints, which may require different approaches in make-up. Photographs can sometimes be larger than life, which will also exploit any imperfection in the make-up. The viewer also has the opportunity to study a photograph closely. As stated earlier, photographers are shooting digitally more often than on film mainly at the request of clients. There is little or no difference between the two formats and most photographs will undergo a touch up process to fix any imperfections. The photographer has now become the processing shop and will usually handle touch ups with the use of a program like Photoshop.

Theater

Theater is the most forgiving of all media. That is not to say that theater make-up is easy, just that the audience is further away than any other viewing audience. The make-up done for a stage production will be more intense, darker colors are used, but the application and techniques are the same as any other medium. The intensity of the make-up will be based on how big the house is and how far the audience is from the stage. An intimate house of only one hundred seats the make-up will be very similar to a film make-up, simple and natural. When creating a make-up design it should be done with the first ten rows in mind, never do a make-up that is meant to be seen from the back of the house. The main difference is that after the characters are designed, the actors put on their own make-up. The make-up artist is responsible for training the actors and then viewing the make-up from the house to ensure that proper application is done. The only exception to this is when dealing with very elaborate make-ups.

GLOSSARY OF TERMS

A

99% Alcohol: Isopropyl alcohol is a colorless, flammable chemical compound with a strong odor. It is commonly used as a cleaner and solvent in the industry. It should be kept away from heat and open flame and used in well-ventilated areas.

Acetone: A colorless, flammable chemical with a distinct smell. It is found in cosmetics and personal care products and is also used to dissolve other substances. It should be kept away from heat and open flame and used in well-ventilated areas.

Acrylic Paint: Can be diluted with water, but become water-resistant when dry. Depending on how much the paint is diluted (with water) or modified with acrylic gels, mediums, or pastes, the finished acrylic painting can resemble a watercolor or an oil painting. It is commonly used by artists and mixed with Pros-aide to make Pax Paint.

Adhesive: A compound that adheres or bonds two items together. Adhesives may come from either natural or synthetic sources.

Age Spots: Collections of pigment caused by exposure to the sun. Bruising that leaves blood pigment behind also can cause age spots. They are most common in people older than 55. The spots commonly appear on the hands, but they can be almost anywhere, especially sun-exposed areas, such as the face, back, arms, feet and shoulders.

Age Stipple: Process of stretching the skin, stippling on a material such as latex powdering the area and releasing the skin. This creates a relatively effective wrinkling effect often indicative of older skin.

Airbrush: A small, air-operated tool that sprays various media including ink and dye, but most often paint by a process of atomization (conversion of bulk liquid into a spray or mist, often by passing the liquid through a nozzle).

Application: The technique used to put a make-up product on the model.

Anchoring Point: A strong spot of adhesive used to hold a bald cap or prosthetic appliance in place.

B

Bald Cap: The name of the appliance used to create the effect of a bald person. Usually made from latex or vinyl plastic.

Bald Cap Form: A form in the shape of a head used to make a bald cap.

Base Color: A flesh tone make-up. This preps skin for flawless make-up application by filling in fine lines and wrinkles.

Base Match: A flesh tone make-up that matches the performer perfectly.

Black Stipple Sponge: A type of sponge with a large cell structure used to create scrapes and beard stubble.

Blister: A small bubble on the skin filled with fluid and caused by heat or friction.

Bondo: Cab-o-sil and Pros-aide mixed together to a creamy paste used to fill in make-up depressions

Brick Color: A red color used as an undertone on prosthetics. Also used to add subtle redness to a face.

Brow Bone: The protrusion of bone that the eyebrow rests upon. In eye shadow treatments, highlight is placed under the eyebrow and along the base of the brow bone.

Bruise: An area of skin discoloration. A bruise occurs when small blood vessels break and leak their contents into the soft tissue beneath the skin. . It begins as a pinkish red and eventually changes to a bluish color, then greenish-yellow, and finally returns to the normal skin color as it heals.

Bullet: A solid projectile propelled by a firearm or air gun and is normally made from metal (usually lead). A bullet does not contain explosives, but damages the intended target by tissue disruption and impact.

Bullet Wound: Wound to the skin caused by sudden impact with a bullet.

Burn: A burn is an injury caused by heat, cold, electricity, chemicals, light, radiation, or friction. Burns can be highly variable in terms of the tissue affected, the severity, and resultant complications.

C

Cab-o-sil: Fumed silica used to make chemicals thicker.

Canister: A container of compressed gas.

Capillaries: A branching blood vessel connecting arteries and veins.

Carbon Dioxide: A non-flammable gas used as an airbrush propellant.

Casting Urethane: a two component liquid system, usually processed by machine dispensing or hand mixing and pouring into an open mold. This offers several advantages, including low mold cost as well as the ability to produce large parts.

Castor Oil: A vegetable oil obtained from the castor bean. Castor oil is a colorless to very pale yellow liquid with mild or no odor or taste.

Cheekbone: Bone below the eye, also known as the zygomatic arch.

Cheek Color: A make-up product that is applied to the center of the cheekbone. It can either be a cream or powdered product.

Clavicle: The clavicle is a doubly curved short bone that connects the arm to the body, located directly above the first rib. It is also known as the Collarbone.

Clay: A naturally occurring material composed primarily of fine-grained minerals, which show plasticity through a variable range of water content, and which can be hardened when dried and/or fired.

Coagulation: When blood changes from a liquid to a semisolid or clot. This is used to sculpt prosthetics.

Compressor: A machine used for compressing air for use with an airbrush.

Construction: The process of building a character on the actor's face.

Contour: The process of highlight and shading that achieves the desired effect, which is to emphasize specific curves and indentations in a make-up application.

Corners of the Mouth: Where the upper and lower lips meet.

Cotton: A soft, staple fiber that grows around the seeds of the cotton plant. The fiber most often is spun into yarn or thread and used to make a soft breathable textile which is the most widely used natural-fiber cloth in clothing today.

Cotton Swabs: Used in first aid, cosmetics application, and a variety of other uses. They consist of a small wad of cotton wrapped around the end of a small rod, made of wood, rolled paper, or plastic. The most common type of usage is to dip the cotton end in a substance, then use the swab as an applicator for the substance.

Coverage: A term used to describe how translucent or how opaque a make-up is.

Crease: A deep line or wrinkle in the face.

Crepe Wool: Wool fibers used to simulate hair.

Crown: This refers to the top of the head, where the bald cap must be aligned.

Crystal Clear Acrylic Coating: Spray coating used to seal sculptures and for spraying on a fake beard when it is applied to a toughie head.

Cupid's Bow: The center area of the upper lip that appears to have two peaks and a valley.

Cut: A tear in the skin.

D

Depth: Deepness, a measurement from the top down.

Dismantle: To take apart.

Dissolve: To turn a solid into a liquid.

Drop Shadow: Used to create the illusion of a thick lower lash line. Can be applied with eye shadow, eye pencil, or liquid liner.

E

Entrance Wound: Point of injury caused by a bullet entering the body.

Epoxy Parafilm: A spray release agent used to de-mold gelatin appliances.

Exit Wound: Injury caused by a bullet leaving the body.

Eyebrow: A group of hairs that grow above the eye, on the brow bone or superscalar arch.

Eyebrow Pencil: A make-up pencil used to shape, define, and fill in the eyebrow

Eye Fold: The space between the upper lid line and under the eyebrow. Folds can either be one of or any combination of the following: slight fold, flat eye, recessed eye, heavy fold, Asian slight fold, or Asian heavy fold.

Eyeliner: A make-up product that is used to shape, adds definition, and enhance the eye. Liquid, pencil, and eye shadow may be used as eyeliners.

Eye shadow: A colored powder make-up used to enhance, highlight, and shade the eyes.

Eye Pencil: A make-up pencil used to shape, define, and enhance the eyes.

F

Face Chart: A chart used to design or maintain the look of a character.

Fatty Tissue: Area above the eye that begins to hang down as we age.

Feathering: To blend something carefully into the skin using the tip of the make-up brush, much like a feather.

Filbert Brush: A rounded and tapered brush typically used to apply eye shadow.

Fixer Spray: A thin sealer used to seal wax constructions and the edge of a vinyl bald cap.

Flashing: The excess material that surrounds an unapplied prosthetic appliance.

Flexible Collodion: Plastic sealer used to seal wax constructions and the edge of a vinyl bald cap.

Flocking: Rayon fibers cut into small pieces and used to color gelatin and silicone.

Foam Latex: A material used to create prosthetic appliances.

Foundation: A make-up product that evens out the skin, toning down slight imperfections and flaws. It also refers to the entire process of base, highlight, shadow, concealer, and powder application.

Frontal Bone: The forehead bone.

Fumed Silica: Silicone dioxide that has been exuded.

G

Gaf-quat: Super strong hair gel.

Gelatin: Transparent jelly-like substance derived from skin, tendons, etc., used in cooking and photography.

Glycerin: A thick, sweet, and colorless liquid used in medicine, ointment, hair products, and cosmetics.

H

Hackle: A piece of wood or metal with a series of closely placed pins, set-up in rows that are used like a giant comb to de-tangle most types of hair.

Hair Punching Needle: A needle used to push hair into artificial skin.

Hair White: A product used to turn normal hair into gray hair.

Hard Edge: A sharp visual division between highlight and shadow.

Hash Marks: Haphazard lines quickly drawn on the face.

Headshot: An 8x10 professional photograph of an actor, usually from the neck up.

Highlight: A light colored or reflective area.

I

Ice Powder: A product used to re-create the effect of ice and snow on the face.

Indented scar: A scar that has created a depression in the skin.

Injury: Harm or damage to the skin.

Ink Blot Pencil: An artist's pencil used to make tattoo transfers on newsprint paper.

Iridescent: Reflects light and has shine.

J

Jagged: Unevenly cut or torn.

Jowl: Fleshy part of the jaw line.

K

Keloid: A type of scar, which results in an overgrowth of tissue at the site of a healed skin injury. Keloids are firm, rubbery lesions or shiny, fibrous nodules, and can vary from pink to flesh-colored or red to dark brown in color.

Knead: To press, fold, and squeeze something.

K-Y Jelly: A brand of personal lubricant used to remove excess powder.

L

Labial Roll: A natural highlight that surrounds the edge of the lips. It adds dimension to the lip.

Lace: A fine, loose-weave material used to tie individual hairs on to make a hairpiece.

Laceration: A tear in the skin.

Latex: Liquid rubber.

Life cast: The process of taking an impression of someone's face or body.

Lip Line: The defined edge that surrounds the upper and lower lip.

Lipstick: A make-up product used to color lips. Lipstick comes in a wide variety of colors, formulas, and finishes.

Lip Gloss: A make-up product for the lips that is thicker than lipstick, and imparts a high shine. Can be worn alone, over lip liner, or over lipstick.

Lip Liner: A make-up pencil used to shape, define, and color lips.

M

Mascara: Eye make-up product that colors, lengthens, and thickens the eyelashes. Available in a variety of colors and formulas.

M.E.K.: Methyl Ethel Ketone; a harsh solvent.

Mandible: Lower jaw of humans.

Matte: Clear make-up finish, has no shine.

Matte Medium: Clear acrylic material used to matte acrylic paint.

Maxillae: Bones that make up the area around the upper and lower teeth.

Mold: A hollow container into which a substance, such as foam latex, is poured or injected.

Morgue: A collection of photographs for the purpose of reference.

Mortician's Wax: A pliable material used as a sculpting material on the face.

Mortuary: A room or building where dead bodies are kept until burial.

Mustard Yellow: A muted yellow color used to add olive to a base color.

N

Naphtha: Lighter fluid; used to help dissolve the edge of a rubber bald cap.

Nasolabial Fold: The crease that runs from above the nostril to just out from the corner of the mouth.

Negative Mold: The mold half that is the reverse shape of a prosthetic appliance.

Nostrils: Either of the two openings of the nose.

Nozzle: The tip of the airbrush.

O

Occipital: The protruding bone on the back of the head.

Olive: A yellow-green color.

Opaque: Impossible to see through, does not allow light to pass through.

Orange Stipple Sponge: A large celled sponge used to stipple color into the skin.

Overlay Drawing: A design traced on paper to help production understand what a character may look like.

P

Paasche: An airbrush manufacturer.

Paint & Powder: Terminology used to describe the process of aging with color.

Palette: A metal, waxed paper, or acrylic piece used as a holding area for make-up.

Palette Knife: Artist's knife used to sculpt wax and to scoop make-up from containers.

Pax Paint: Pros-aide, acrylic paint, and matte medium mixed together to make a very sticky paint for prosthetics.

Photoshop: A computer program used to alter photographs for design reasons.

Pigment: Coloring matter usually in powder form and mixed with oils, water, etc. to create a colored make-up.

Pigmented Powder: Talc and pigment mixed together to form a translucent powder.

Plastic Beard: A beard made on a toughie head and sprayed with a plastic spray for the purpose of removing the beard and re-applying it to an actor.

Plastic Sealer: Sealer used to seal wax constructions and the edge of a vinyl bald cap.

Plastic Spray: Spray coating used to seal sculptures and for spraying on a fake beard when it is applied to a toughie head.

Pliatex Mold Rubber: Latex used for making bald caps and molds.

Powder: Talc that is used for setting make-up and decreasing shine.

Powder Puff: A velour pad used to hold powder.

Primary Colors: Red, blue, and yellow.

Producer: The maker of the movie, and usually the person funding it.

Production: Term used to describe the phase of filmmaking where shooting takes place; commercial, movie, music video, etc.

Pros-Aide: A white acrylic adhesive used to apply prosthetics. It dries clear.

Prosthetic Appliance: Foam latex, gelatin, or silicone piece used to change the features of an actor's face.

R

Rayon Flocking: Fibers cut into small pieces and used to color gelatin and silicone.

Release Agent: A separator for molds and prosthetics.

Rigid Collodion: A material used to create indented scars.

Roughing Out: Terminology used to describe the first steps of sculpting where the design of the character is created.

Rubber: A tough elastic substance made from latex of plants or synthetically.

Rubber Cement: A common type of glue used to mix with pigment in order to create a paint that will stick to urethane foams.

Rubber Mask Grease Paint: Castor oil based cream make-up designed for use on all rubber products.

Ruddy: A reddish undertone.

S

Scar: An old healed cut.

Scrape: An injury to the skin caused by friction.

Scratch: A small cut.

Sculpture: The art of making three-dimensional forms using clay.

Shade: The value of lightness/darkness of a color.

Shadow: To darken or cast by an object between a light source and a subject.

Shine: A highly reflective spot or area caused by moisture or perspiration.

Sideburn: Facial hair in front of the ears.

Silicone Adhesive: Medical grade adhesive which uses silicone and solvents as its base. It is durable, flexible, and resistant to moisture and often times costly.

Silicone Caulk: Clear caulk used to seal windows and bathtubs. We use it as a paint system for silicone skins.

Silicone G.F.A.: Silicone Gel filled appliances, the most recent advance in prosthetics.

Skin Illustrator: A brand of alcohol based make-up.

Skin Tone: The color of skin. Usually a combination of shade and undertone mixed to match a person's skin color.

Slip: A term used in cosmetics to describe the consistency of a liquid or cream product. The more slip a product has, the creamier it feels.

Soft Edge: The gradation between highlight and shadow.

Sorbitol: A preservative used in gelatin appliances that increase strength and stability.

Special Make-up Effects: Term used to describe make-up and effects that are not traditional forms of make-up application.

Spirit Gum: A resin-based adhesive used mainly for hair work.

Stagey: An overly done make-up application.

Stipple: The process of applying make-up and the dotted pattern left by that process.

Sunburn: Burn caused by overexposure to the sun.

Swelling: A raised injury to the skin.

Symmetry: Perfect balance between two sides.

Synthetic Hair: Artificially created hair usually made of plastic fiber.

T

Taper: To diminish as it moves away.

Tattoo: Permanent art on the skin.

Tattoo Ink: Alcohol based colors used to re-create tattoos.

Tear Duct: The duct in the innermost corner of the eye where tears are formed.

Telesis: A brand name of silicone adhesive.

Telesis Thinner: Product used to thin or lessen the strength of Telesis.

Three-Dimensional: Having height, depth and width.

Tuffie Head: A face made of firm urethane used to practice beard applications.

Translucent: Allowing light to pass through.

Transparent: Completely clear, able to see through.

Tuplast: A thick plastic material used to create blisters and scars.

Tweezers: A small tool used for grabbing small items.

Two-Dimensional: Having height and width, no depth.

U

Ultra Ice: Product designed to look like ice on the skin.

Undertone: The underlying color of the skin.

Urethane: Water-soluble crystalline compound.

V

Vehicle: The material that transports pigment. It is the element of make-up that gives it slip.

Veins: Any of the tubes conveying blood to the heart.

Ventilate: The process of hand-tying each hair to lace.

Ventilating Needle: The needle used in ventilating (the process of hand tying each hair to lace).

Vinyl: Plastic material used to make bald caps.

Viscosity: Refers to the thickness of a liquid.

Volatile: Evaporates easily.

W

Wax: A pliable material used as a sculpting material on the face.

White Sponge: A foam sponge used to apply make-up to a performer.

Witch Hazel: A mild astringent used to remove make-up and other products from the skin.

Woochie: A brand name of low cost latex appliances.

Wound: Injury to the skin.

Wrinkles: Lines and creases in the face caused by aging.

Y

Yak Hair: A Yak is a large domesticated wild Tibetan Ox with long, shaggy and bulky hair.

Z

Zinc Oxide: White pigment.

Zygomatic Arch: The Cheekbone

PROFESSIONAL MAKE-UP SUPPLIERS

The following stores provide make-up materials to the professional make-up artist.
Some of these companies additionally provide student discounts.

Alcone
5-45 49th Ave.
Lond Island City, NY 11101
Phone: (718) 361-8373

Alcone NYC
322 W.49th St..
New York, NY 10019
Phone: (212) 757-3734
alconeco.com

Burman Industries
13536 Saticoy St.
Van Nuys, CA 91402
Phone: (818) 782-9833
burmanfoam.com

Cinema Secrets
4400 Riverside Drive
Burbank, CA 91505
Phone: (718) 361-8373
cinemascrets.com

Davis Dental/Cinema FX
7347 Ethel Ave.
N. Hollywood, CA 91605
Phone: (818) 765-4994
fxsupplies.com

Industry Cosmetics & Beauty Supply Inc.
546 Yonge Street
Toronto, ON M4Y 1Y8
(416) 925-0462
industrycosmetics.com

Frends Beauty Supply
5270 Laurel Canyon Blvd.
N. Hollywood, CA 91607
Phone: (818) 769-3834

FX Warehouse
Phone: (386) 254-0497
fxwarehouse.info

M.A.P.
6 Goldhawk Mews
Shepherds Bush
London W12 8PA
+44 (0) 20 8740 0808
makeup-provisions.com

Media Makeup
Mezzanine Level, Shop 17,
Renaissance Arcade
Pulteney Street Adelaide South
Australia 5000
(08) 8223 3233
mediamakeup.com.au

Motion Picture FX Co.
123 S. Victory Blvd.
Burbank, CA 91502
Phone: (818) 563-2366
makeupkits.com

Mudshop – LA
129 S. San Fernando Blvd.
Burbank, CA 91502
Phone: (818) 557-7619
mudshop.com

Mudshop – NYC
375 West Broadway
New York, NY 10012
Phone: (212) 925-9250
mudshop.com

Naimie's Beauty Supply
12640 Riverside Drive
N. Hollywood, CA 91606
Phone: (818) 655-9922
naimies.com

Nigel's Beauty Emporium
11252 Magnolia Blvd
North Hollywood, CA 91601
(818) 760-3902
nigelsbeautysupply.com

Special Effects Supply Co.
164 E. Center St.
North Salt Lake, UT 84054
Phone: (801) 936-9762
fxsupply.com

RECOMMENDED REFERENCE AND MAKE-UP BOOKS

Make-up Designory's Beauty Make-up
by Yvonne Hawker and John Bailey.   Make-up Designory,
Burbank, California 2004   ISBN 0-9749500-1-7

Stage Makeup, Eighth Edition, by Richard Corson. Prentice-
Hall, Englewood Cliffs, New Jersey, 1986   ISBN 0-13-840521-2

Fashions In Makeup, by Richard Corson.
Peter Owen Limited, London   ISBN 0-7206-0431-1

Fashions In Hair, by Richard Corson.
Peter Owen Limited, London   ISBN 0-7206-3283-8

*The Technique of the Professional Make-up for Film,
Television and Stage,* by Vincent J-R Kehoe.
Focal Press, Boston 1985   ISBN 0-240-51244-8

Special Makeup Effects, by Vincent J-R Kehoe.
Focal Press, Boston 1991   ISBN 0-240-80099-0

Techniques of Three Dimensional Make-up, by Lee
Baygan. Watson-Guptill Publications,
New York 1988   ISBN 0-8230-5261-3

The Complete Make-up Artist, by Penny Delamar.
Northwestern University Press,
Evanston 1997   ISBN 0-8101-1258-2

*Making Faces:
A Complete Guide to Face Painting,* by Sian Ellis-Thomas
Sunburst Books, London   ISBN 1-85778-238-0

The Art of Make-up, by Kevyn Aucoin. Harper Collins
Publishers, Callaway Editions 1994   ISBN 0-06-017186-3

Making Faces, by Kevyn Aucoin. Little, Brown & Company,
Boston 1997   ISBN 0-316-28686-9

*Fine Beauty: Beauty Basics and Beyond
for African-American Women,* by Sam Fine. Riverhead
Books, New York 1998   ISBN 1-57322-095-7

Hollywood Glamour Portraits, by John Kobal (editor).
Dover Publications, New York, 1976   ISBN 0-486-23352-9

*Behind The Mask: The Secrets of Hollywood's
Monster Masks,* by Mark Salisbury and Alan Hedgecock.
Titan Books, London, 1994   ISBN 1-85286-488-5

*Men, Makeup and Monsters: Hollywood's Masters
of Illusion and FX,* by Anthony Timpone. St. Martin's Press,
New York, 1996   ISBN 0-312-14678-7

Do It Yourself - Monster Makeup Handbook, by
Dick Smith. Imagine, Inc., Pittsburgh 1985 ISBN 0-911137-02-5

How To Draw Animals, by Jack Hamm. Perigee Books
Putnam Publishing Group, New York   ISBN 0-399-50802-3

After Ninety, by Imogen Cunningham.
(paperback)   ISBN 0-295-95673-9

Barlowe's Guide to Fantasy, by Wayne Douglas Barlowe.
(paperback)   ISBN 0-06-100817-6

The Source Book: Props, Set Dressing & Wardrobe,
Debbie's Book, 2000   ISBN 0-9637404-6-6

Drawing on the Right Side of the Brain,
by Betty Edwards. Jeremy P. Tarcher, Inc. ISBN 0-87477-523-X

The Mane Thing, by Kevin Mancuso. ISBN 0-316-166-146

Drawing the Human Head, by Burne Hogarth.
Watson-Guptill Publications   ISBN 0-8230-1375-8

An Atlas of Anatomy for Artists,
by Fritz Schider. Dover Publication, Inc.   ISBN 486-20241-0

Gray's Anatomy, by Henry Gray, F.R.S. ISBN 0-914294-49-0

1940's Hairstyles, by Daniela Turudich.
Streamline Press   ISBN 930064-01-2

Film and Television Makeup, by Herman Buchman.
Watson-Guptill Publications   ISBN 0-8230-7560-50

The Face is a Canvas, by Irene Corey.
Anchorage Press, Inc.   ISBN 087602-031-7

Faces Fantasy Makeup, by Martin Jans and
Servaas Van Eijk.   ISBN 90-70659-03-4

Assoline, by Serge Lutens.   ISBN 2-84323-066-7

Il Trucco E La Mashero, by Stefano Anselmo.
                                               ISBN 88-85278-10-8

Art & Fear, by David Bayles & Ted Orland.
Capra Press   ISBN 0-88496-379-9

Magazines

Make up Artist Magazine

On Makeup Magazine

Cinefantastique

Rue Morgue

Daily Variety

Hollywood Reporter

Mercury Production Report

Allure

Marie Claire

Instyle

Inspire Quarterly

Modern Salon

American Salon

Elle

Cosmopolitan

Classes & Products

Make-up Designory, the largest make-up school in the nation, was founded over a decade ago to bring excellence to make-up education. Accomplished professional make-up artisans, who share a passion for creating an inspirational learning environment, teach our students practical and sophisticated skills. With two thriving campuses in Los Angeles and New York, students from around the world join us to study beauty make-up artistry, hairstyling, character and special make-up effects. We've graduated some of the finest make-up artists in the industry into "starring roles" – from Hollywood to Broadway and the runways of Europe.

Out of this unparalleled educational program, we've created our superb Make-Up Designory line of make-up and tools. We've evolved a friendly, accessible approach to educating everyday users on how to look their best with our products, so that they can become make-up experts themselves. It's a high standard of make-up offered with a clear, instructional approach that you won't find anywhere else.

Make-up Designory classes are offered year-round, with day and evening schedules available.

- Beauty Make-up Artistry
- Character Make-up Artistry
- Special Make-up Effects
- Studio Hairstyling
- Portfolio Development
- Fashion Make-up Artistry
- Journeyman Make-up Artistry
- Master Make-up Artistry
- Make-up II
- Make-up III

For more information or to request a school catalog, please visit www.mud.edu or call 818-729-9420 (Los Angeles) or 212-925-9250 (New York).

To purchase MUD products, visit one of our retailers or MUD shops.

MUD Shop Los Angeles
129 S. San Fernando Blvd.
Burbank, CA 91502
818-729-9420

MUD Shop New York
375 W. Broadway
New York, NY 10012
212-925-9250

For a complete list of retail locations, please visit www.mudshop.com

AN EDUCATED APPROACH TO MAKE-UP.™   mudshop.com | mud.edu